SOMEBODY'S CHILD

SOMEBODY'S CHILD

Stories from the Private Files of an Adoption Attorney

RANDI G. BARROW, ESQ.

A Perigee Book

A Perigee Book
Published by The Berkley Publishing Group
A division of Penguin Putnam Inc.
375 Hudson Street
New York, New York 10014

First Perigee edition: October 2002

Visit our website at www.penguinputnam.com

Library of Congress Cataloging-in-Publication Data

Barrow, Randi.
Somebody's child : stories from the private files of an adoption attorney / Randi Barrow.
p.   cm.
ISBN 0-399-52816-4
1. Adoption—United States—Case studies.   2. Adoptive parents—United States—
Biography.   3. Birthmothers—United States—Biography.   I. Title.

HV875.55 .B365   2002
362.73'4'0973—dc21
2002025281

Printed in the United States of America

10   9   8   7   6   5   4   3   2   1

This book is dedicated with love and gratitude to my mother,

Dorothy Pitzer

Contents

Acknowledgments   ix
Introduction   xi
Epigraph   xvii

1. The Baby Who Wasn't There   1
   ELIZABETH AND TOM, adoptive parents

2. A Grandmother's Tale   35
   AMELIA, a birthgrandmother

3. The Phantom Father   69
   COLLEEN, a birthmother

4. "Where's Mommy?"   81
   PAUL AND MARC, adoptive parents

5. Not So Black and White   107
   PATRICE, an adoptive mother

6. Why Don't They Want My Baby?   127
   MICHELLE, a birthmother

Contents

7. Where Do Babies Come From?   151
   BOBBI, a birthmother

8. Childless Mother, Motherless Child   175
   JANE, a birthmother

9. A New American Family   203
   GLORIA, an adoptive mother

10. Never Too Old   227
    MICKEY, an adoptive father

11. Three's a Charm   249
    SUSAN, an adoptive mother

12. Rethinking Adoption   277

Acknowledgments

LONG BEFORE THIS book, there was law school. Without the help of my husband, Arthur Barrow, I could never have managed those three years. I might not have jumped into solo practice without the encouraging words of my brother, Greg Pitzer. Once I opened an office, I could not have survived without the bravery of those first adoptive parents who hired me despite my inexperience. I am grateful to all the adoptive parents who have allowed me to share their adoptions with them.

For her help and acceptance, especially in those early years, I thank Felice Webster, a skilled and caring adoption attorney. To Nikki Biers of the Adoption Circle, many thanks for the camaraderie, and the wonderful job you do. To every birth-mother I have ever worked with, thank you for making adoption possible.

To the hardworking adoption service providers, and the underappreciated social workers at the Department of Children and Family Services, and Vista Del Mar Child and Family Services, thank you for your dedicated service. To the clerks at the Edmund D. Edelman Children's Court, who know more than all of us, thank you. To Judge John L. Henning: None of us could accomplish our goals in adoption without your kindness and wisdom.

To the members of the Academy of California Adoption Lawyers and the American Academy of Adoption Attorneys, thank you for setting high standards and working to make adoption the best it can be.

To all of those who agreed to be interviewed for this book, my respect and gratitude for your courage. To anyone I imposed upon to read a chapter or two of this book as it developed, especially my mother, my thanks. To Lisa Loomer, a remarkable writer, thank you for seeing something that made you want to share these stories with a wider audience.

Without Charlotte Gusay, literary agent extraordinaire, I would not have had a tireless advocate working her hardest to get this book published. Without Sheila Curry Oakes, a fine and perceptive editor, and her belief in this book, it would still be a manuscript in a drawer.

With their help, and the support of my husband, family, and friends, I pushed on until the mass of notes, tapes, and ideas became *Somebody's Child*. To all of them, my deepest thanks.

Introduction

THE SUBJECT OF adoption brings forth universal, primal questions: Who am I? Where did I come from? Where do I belong? Adoption as a secret event with sealed records and changed identities is a product of this century. There were no laws governing adoption in the United States until Massachusetts passed the first adoption statute in 1851. The closing of adoption records began in 1917 and was solidly in place in most states by the late 1930s. The rationale behind this campaign was the protection of the mother and the child from what was then considered the stigma of illegitimacy. It was not until the 1970s that things began to change as society's values regarding illegitimacy and single parenthood evolved. What the American public thinks of as a "normal" adoption is actually a historical aberration, practiced for a period of only fifty or sixty years.

Adoption has come a long way from the practices of the first half of the twentieth century, from the cruel institutions that condemned women and gave their children to people they did not choose and could never know. Current adoption practice gives the birthmother the absolute right to determine the fate of her child, even if her choice is not beneficial to herself or to her child. The viewpoint has shifted far away from state and societal concerns of illegitimacy to an expression of individual choice. A pregnant girl of fourteen years is allowed to make an adoption decision unimpeded by the desires of her family, although that same girl may not vote or drive a car.

The evolution away from paternalistic control and disapproval of the state is the single most important change in adoption, and is to be applauded, but the changes have come unevenly, with some outstanding inequities still in place. Consider the following:

In some states a birthmother may change her mind about the adoption for several months after the baby is in the adoptive parents' home.

She may keep any money given to her and doesn't have to repay it even if she changes her mind.

A birthfather who has beaten the birthmother is still granted rights under the law.

The state prevents those with certain criminal records from adopting, yet provides conjugal visits for convicted felons.

Agreements promising birthmothers photos or visits are generally unenforceable.

In most states gays and lesbians are forbidden to adopt as couples, and in some states may not adopt at all.

★   ★   ★

WE ARE A country that prides itself on our concern for children, for the underdog and the little guy. But not much of that concern has made its way into adoption law and practice. Children languish in foster care until they are "unadoptable"; those with little money have little chance of adopting a newborn. And that's the short list. It's time for a change.

It is popular in some circles to say that adoption used to be about the welfare of the children and that now it is about fulfilling the desires of infertile couples. It is, of course, about the welfare of the child, the adoptive family, and the birthmother; it is about cooperation. It is not an adversarial process. There is no need to take sides in adoption; one does not need to be for birthparents and against adoptive parents, or vice versa. The point is to see our common ground and to ask the law to rearrange itself around the real needs of the participants.

As an adoption attorney, I've had the privilege of holding a woman's hand and comforting her during labor while frantic adoptive parents drove hundreds of miles to be at her side. Birthmothers I barely knew shared the burdens of their lives and their secret longings with me. I've watched as birthfathers hesitated, and then, sometimes in tears, put pen to paper and gave away their parental rights. Whatever I thought I understood about life before I worked in adoption was magnified and intensified a thousandfold.

I didn't stumble into adoption accidentally. For years my husband and I endured the emotional strain and physical trauma of infertility treatments. I finally realized that my experiences were meant to prepare me to help others through adoption, not to be a mother myself. My only regret is that it took me so long to figure this out; I would love to have skipped operations one, two, and three, and those wicked medications that rearrange your body and soul. But as the Chinese say, the only way around something is all the way through it.

Before I had been practicing adoption law a full year, I began to lay the groundwork for this book. I found myself compelled to interview birthmothers, to tape and preserve their stories, without knowing what I would do with them. I would bring my handheld tape recorder to a coffee shop and question a woman about the most personal issues in her life while waitresses and busboys swirled around us. Sometimes people came to my office, sometimes I recorded them over the phone.

Interviews with adoptive parents helped complete my picture of adoption in the United States today. What happened to birthparents and adoptive parents between conception and adoption encompassed a universe of human drama and experience. After many years, these interviews, and my own frustration with the adoption system, came together to form this book.

The interviews, which have been edited to form a narrative in people's own words describing their adoption experience, do not talk only about that experience, but lead us through each person's life, showing the personal history behind his or her decision. A few of these experiences could be considered extreme or unusual. I have included them here to give the broadest possible perspective on adoption. In editing the interviews, I tried to remain true to each story, deleting only my questions and repetitive or peripheral material, and adding a word here and there for clarity.

In a short commentary at the end of each chapter, I use each person's story to illustrate important adoption topics. I highlight some of the legal, moral, and practical questions they pose, including birthfathers' rights, money given to birthmothers, and what happens when a birthmother changes her mind.

In the commentaries and throughout the book, I have purposefully avoided, where possible, citing statutes and statistics. I want to convey a more personal understanding of adoption, using the words of the participants themselves to provide the most moving and vivid illustration of how badly change is needed. In this book you will meet Colleen, who tells us the true story of her pregnancy four years *after* the birth of her son. You'll also meet Bobbi, who claims not to have had intercourse: "I'm in a statistics book; the doctor wrote it down." And Patrice, whose birthmother had sex with an African-American man and had to place her baby for adoption or leave town. Then there is Gloria, who began life as a man named Jorge, and went on to adopt four times. "Even if I am a fake woman, I am a great woman for kids." These are just some of the men and women who open their lives and hearts to us.

My purpose in offering these stories and my comments is to see our mostly outdated, unfair adoption system torn down and built anew. I am not shy in my criticism of adoption laws and practices, and I have strong beliefs about how they must be changed. I want this book to be an instrument of that change through the information and, I hope, inspiration it provides. I also want to help banish prejudices, stereotypes, and ignorance; I want all of us to rethink our ideas and attitudes about adoption. The last chapter offers a vision and a plea for a more reasonable and modern adoption system.

"Tell them we're not monsters!" a birthmother once said to me as I was preparing to speak to a roomful of preadoptive parents. There is a need in those interviewed here and others like them to be heard, for their stories to matter, for their opinions to have an effect, for someone to care. They spoke from their hearts and their experiences, risking their privacy, revealing facts of which they were not proud, enduring the pain of remembrance, just so someone might read their words and understand.

The goal of this book is to create a deeper understanding of adoption and a blueprint for change. My hope, too, is that it will create discussion, and encourage people to rethink adoption and approach it with a more educated and open mind and heart. If it inspires one person to stop before asking a birthmother, "How could you give your baby away?" or another to pause before infusing those wanting to adopt with baseless fears, I will have made progress toward that goal.

"Give me children, or else I die."

Rachel—Genesis 30:1

1

The Baby Who Wasn't There

ELIZABETH AND TOM

Adoptive parents

"I know they all say this, but now that I'm here on the other side of it, yeah, it was all worth it."

I must have been about twenty-four or so. We'd been married for about a year and I started having all sorts of pelvic aches and pains. I went in for surgery—it turned out that it was endometriosis. They took it out, because it was not going to get any better. The doctor told me it would probably come back, but we had at least five years before it was something to worry about. Within nine months I started having the same kind of pains. I said, "It's back." They looked at me like, "No, no, you can't be right." I started referring to the whole thing as a vet-pet relationship, as opposed to doctor-patient. I might as well have been barking at them for as much as they would listen to me. They finally said, "Yeah, I guess you're right."

After my surgery we were very active. We got a plane, and

we both got our pilot's licenses and were doing aerobatics training, hiking, all those things that, I guess, you can't really do if you have kids. None of our friends were having children either. Some of our best friends were gay couples, so it wasn't exactly like there was pressure there. Nobody was hearing their clock ticking in any way.

We didn't really start looking into adoption until after we rolled our Bronco out in Arizona. Just outside of Holbrook we both fell asleep in the car—it was the middle of the afternoon—and rolled the Bronco. We refer to it as being the "spin cycle" on the Bronco. All of our stuff went flying out, and fortunately neither of us were really hurt. But it's when we looked back to that trip that we kind of woke up. We kept joking that if we'd had kids in the car they would have kept nagging us about "when we were going to be there" and we probably would have stayed awake.

Up to that point we'd always said, "Yes, if we want a family we'll adopt," and that was that. There really was no urgency for us to go through the adoption process either. There was no deadline. There wasn't much pressure from our parents. It was after we came back from that trip that we went to the county's adoption orientation meeting, checking into what was available. We had the real nice social worker that came and talked to everyone. He reminded me of Geraldo, and he was, I thought, very realistic. He said, "If you're looking to adopt a nice, normal, healthy child, you're in the wrong place." We went, Oh well, at least he's laying it out on the line for us. It was two years waiting for an answer, and then five years before you might have a child placed, which at that point seemed like a long way around.

We got out the phone book and made some calls. We were looking for what no longer existed, from what I can tell: orphanages. See, Tom went to a Catholic school and one of the many good deeds they did as students was to visit all the orphanages in town and do plays, make meals, and play with the kids, that kind of thing. They did that quite often. So he remembered that there were kids like that available and who could use someone like us right now. That was the naive story that we had in our heads.

We were never looking particularly for a newborn, we were just open to almost anything. I remember going through lists and making blind calls. We were still shopping around as to where we were going to park ourselves to work on an adoption. One of the guys that I worked with was using a well-known attorney. The whole department seemed to think it was a rather shady deal. I had this prejudice that I didn't want to use an attorney, and I certainly didn't want to go through what he was going through.

At that point we stumbled across an adoption agency and went in for one of those very nice, hopeful meetings, and they explain to you what it will be like to adopt, and if you're ready to adopt and all. They did a home study for us and they were supposed to set us up for an international adoption, probably through Hong Kong, and we were supposed to end up in about two years with a child. Our counselor suggested that she had a friend who dealt with a lot of the Japanese adoption business. She sent us to Linda.

We met Linda a couple weeks before Christmas. What was supposed to be an hour meeting turned out to be a three-hour meeting. Because you go through all these meetings and every time you meet someone new who's going to help you with adoption, you sit there and you nod your head. You're being really polite and very social and always thinking, OK, maybe this one's going to help you out.

Linda called herself a facilitator—she didn't call herself an agency. There were a lot of papers she handed over to us that were mostly from other attorneys or agencies that she'd collected, a lot of stuff you could pick up anywhere. But she also did make us sign that we were not expecting anything out of her, that this was not a fully legal transaction where "We pay our money and she gets us a baby" kind of thing. We gave her $250, which was a consultation fee. She was going to help us with the procedure of international adoption and also try to find us a child if it was available. She also had these two books, big, fat computer-generated directories of doctors in Japan and Asia, attorney listings in Japan that dealt with adoption, things like that. It looked very, very helpful. She was implying that she might be able to come up with something before Hong Kong.

We felt, Well, if the agency says this woman is OK . . . you know? See, from the adoptive parent's point of view, you want to look good to everybody, you don't want to make any enemies, you want to say yes to everything so you don't feel like you're losing a chance anywhere. And if there is any light that you see that you might be able to reach into, you go for it. This story about Linda at that point was a big plus for us. Here was someone who had the Japanese connection and supposedly dealt with that side of the world quite a bit. She fit our needs. Tom was born and raised in Yokohama, Japan. His mother is Japanese, his birthfather is Chinese. To him, Linda looked like she was a mixed race, some Asian and Caucasian. She never really declared what she was.

She was really eager to have us fill out her paperwork—that was the big thing. She wanted to have our paperwork done and put it in her files and then if something came up she could help us out. She didn't promise anything really. She was fairly low-key about the whole thing. I didn't feel like I was being particularly worked over by her at that point. We thought Linda was kind of neat. She was this petite lady who seemed very businesslike but was very friendly. I think that's how we kind of got suckered in. We were desperate too, thinking, Oh, this will be perfect—you know? Her fees were not very expensive, compared to what other people were asking for. So we felt, Well, that's not too bad and we're getting all this information and we're heading in the right direction. She seemed to imply that she had quite a few cases going on and so we were going to see something fairly quickly. After hearing about the two-year wait from Hong Kong, this looked very promising.

A little over a month later she called, and that's when she came up with the story about the two-week-old baby girl. It was pretty much exactly everything we were looking for. The birthmom was Japanese and was a student in chefs' school, the birthfather was Caucasian. The little girl was born with a problem and she had been turned down by other couples because of this club foot. We were all excited—this sounded great. We talked to a couple of doctors first to see what club foot would eventually entail, but it was pretty encouraging. There was going to be some surgery required, but it'll be OK. It just didn't seem like it was that severe, and in fact we were kind of surprised that other people were turning this down and Linda's kind of like, "Well, you know, some of these people want perfect children and that's it."

There was always this urgency, which we've seen in every adoption. Gotta get there, gotta get in, gotta do it. We got a full dose of it on this one. There were a lot of phone calls trying to find out information about us. Linda was doing all the calling in between. The birthmother wanted to know what we wanted to name the baby. We decided we wanted to name her Alexandria. Of course now the joke is, it's a good thing we started off with the "A" names. Linda called back an hour later and said how excited the birthmother was. She said that when she first mentioned the name there was dead silence on the phone. She was kind of worried, Uh-oh, did I offend her in any way? But then she realized that she was so excited because that's what *she* had wanted to name her. There was an old lady who was a candy striper in the hospital that had really helped the birthmother out and knit little booties and all for her, and her name was Alexandria, and the birthmother wanted to name her after her. So I'm going, Oh man, this must be it. We were hooked in good.

This started on a Tuesday and we were all supposed to meet at the agency on Saturday morning. We arranged for an interpreter to be there; we had everyone lined up. That Friday night there was a plane crash at LAX. The next morning about eight o'clock Linda called, and at first she kind of started to tie it into that because she said she'd been calling the birthmother all night and she hadn't been able to get ahold of her. She thought maybe they might have come down early or something. But it turned out that the baby was living with the birthmother's friend in Marin County because the birthmother didn't want to get attached to the baby that much. The friend had put her down for a nap around four-thirty on Friday afternoon. She went to fix dinner, and she went back in later and found her dead.

We had to get on the phone and call everyone and tell everyone that everything's off. I mean, our friends were lined up to bring stuff over. I think our phone didn't stop ringing all weekend long. About a week later we were talking to Linda and we gave her $100 to cover her efforts on this and we also gave her $100 to send flowers to the mother and to the friends who were taking care of the baby. Linda turned around and sent *us* flowers.

The thing the birthmother wanted to do, which was really weird, she wanted to put the birth certificate in our names, with our last name on it. I said, "No, we didn't adopt the child, I don't want to do that. If you put that child's birth certificate in our name there's a possibility we'd end up being responsible for hospital bills." We did offer to help out a little with mortuary costs but there wasn't going to be much, more like cremation or something. Linda made this big thing about the birthfather's father being a chemist, and he supplied chemicals to the mortuary so there wouldn't be any charge for that, he was going to do all that for free, and they were going to send the ashes to us. We were in tears.

Linda said that the birthmother felt so bad, that she really wanted to stay in touch with us, and that she was going to send us a letter or a book or something. She kept saying that the birthmother was going to send us a package but she had the wrong address, so that's why it didn't come to us, it came to Linda. She unwrapped it and gave me everything. We got a real assortment of goodies; it was kind of like a Cracker Jack box prize. There was a pink plastic, heart-shaped box that held the ashes of the baby. The birthmother wrote a note that she was really sorry, she thought the ashes were really discolored. Never having scattered ashes before, you know, you could have fooled me. She said she'd taken it out of the box that came from the mortuary because she didn't think it looked good, so that's why it was in this heart-shaped box. I'm sure now they were fireplace ashes.

Then there was a book that was put together that had pictures of the baby. I suspect there's about three kids in this book. Then there's a lock of hair and there's what's supposed to be the baby's footprints. It's the thing where you use the side of your hand and dab your fingers around it for toes. I went through a few pages of the book and I didn't even want to look at it, I just wanted to put the thing away. It really bothered me.

Then there was also a little bouquet of pink and white silk flowers, a silk scarf, a little piece of traditional Japanese art-work, there was a little vase. There were some real nice things; we could build a shrine out of what we were sent, and I think that's what we were supposed to do. In fact, what we did is we rented some snowshoes and drove up to Big Bear. I'd been up there the year before with a friend and I knew where this area was that was kind of nice. So we went up there and we found a place on the hillside where there was this big stone outcropping, and we put the ashes there. We took some flowers, said a prayer, took a couple of pictures, and traipsed back down. The thing that I have to explain to people is, while you're going through it, it's like a dream because you have the same reactions as though this child really existed and then died.

I did write a letter to the birthmom. Linda didn't have a current address for her . . . she was always moving, that was it. I gave the pictures and letter to Linda. She looked over the pictures and she was, Oh my God, this is so great, you picked such a wonderful spot, and on and on. She was really laying it on thick that we were really such a great couple and we were so understanding. She asked me if I suffered from "Empty Arms Syndrome." I'm thinking, What the heck is this woman talking about? I just kept nodding my head and going along, thinking maybe we'll eventually get a real kid out of this.

We got several letters from the birthmother. They were poorly typed, but it was like, she would write things that looked like someone was trying to pretend they didn't know how to write English, but they did. A lot of incomplete sentences, bad misspellings, and always apologizing in the letter for not being able to do things better. In one letter she said that a nurse that was a friend of hers in Japan was looking for another baby for us, and she was hoping to see us. She was going to come visit us in June. In these letters she was always referring to "our daughter." At this point we were starting to separate from this whole thing. We always felt it was a little too much emphasis that it was "our daughter" and we never actually met her. The letters seemed very strange to us, and as they came along we got less attached to them. We were trying, emotionally, to get away from it.

Linda would always ask if you're interested in adopting siblings. We said yes, so it was time for the sibling story! A U.S. officer was killed in action. His wife was a Japanese journalist; she'd suffered head injuries in a car crash and was in a coma. They had a two-year-old daughter who had a broken leg and spleen damage, but was probably going to recover, and this baby boy who was delivered after the accident. They were checking next of kin—no one in the father's family was interested. The mother's family had disowned her because she had married a Caucasian. We said, "That sounds kind of interesting."

Two days later I got another call from her that we had to get our paperwork together immediately. There was a court date in Japan—it could be as soon as a week. I was concerned about the cost of the two children and she said it was going to come close to $20,000, plus possible other factors. Tom and I looked at each other and said, "We don't have that kind of money, there's no way." She said, "Don't worry, there's another couple who's interested in them." I really felt relieved after saying no. I'm going to only assume that we would have had to pay the fees to *her,* because up to this point all contact was through her.

That's when she started working me over with the next kid, which was this nine-year-old boy. He's local, and she wanted to know if we were interested in pursuing that. We said, "Sure, why not." His name was Nori; he lived with his grandmother, who was dying, and she was his legal guardian. It just so happened that he came from Yokohama, Japan, Tom's hometown. He carried a clarinet wherever he went. His grandmother had a stroke and now was put in a rest home or hospital, so he really did not have a place to go at that point. He was living with a friend of the grandmother's. Linda suggested I call a woman in the Bay Area who used to work for the same law firm she had worked for. She might have information on Nori.

After speaking to the Bay Area facilitator I found out that she knew very little about him. She didn't have information on file, but she said, casually, that Linda seemed to have very few actual adoptions completed. Linda then visited with the foster mother at her apartment. Nori was supposed to stay in the backyard while they discussed the adoption. Linda said he would continuously run in the room, interrupt the conversation. Linda made an appointment for a psychiatrist to evaluate the boy. They were concerned that Nori might have some emotional problems—he was present when his mother committed suicide, that was it. We were supposed to pay for his evaluation, but we never received a bill or a report. We kept saying, "Have you got a report for us?" We never saw the report, so consequently we never got a bill. Meanwhile, there was a Japanese lady who had some dealings with Nori. If there were any questions, or anything more we'd like to know about him, then I could talk to her. Tom talked to her in Japanese and we got a little more information but nothing more than we already knew. That was the third person we talked to—that made it more legit.

The grandmother couldn't speak anymore—she'd had a stroke. They had to have the legal people go to the rest home to do all the paperwork for the adoption. They used a chalk-board, and by nodding of the head or whatever they got this whole paperwork done. The father was an international law attorney and Linda thought he was probably living on the East Coast, but he was calling the foster mother. He wouldn't tell her exactly where he was calling from. She thought he was probably in a hospital. He would ask questions about Nori, but he didn't really want to talk to him.

Then comes one of these panic days. Linda calls up, said this detective showed up at her residence and he wanted information about her and her relationship with us. He also wanted to know what interest we had in the boy. She thought it had something to do with the deposition she was supposed to give. Linda asked us if we were scared and wanted to back out. We said no, carefully, not wanting to be involved in a custody battle with the birthfather. She went to the deposition. She asked me if I wanted to go along, but I thought, No, it might jeopardize my case. She met the attorney. He was with a woman assistant and the detective that showed up at her residence. They asked her the same questions the detective had asked her before concerning the little boy and the relationship to us and our intentions. Linda asked in turn if the birthfather planned to take custody of the boy, and the answer was no. Linda went ahead and filed the completed paperwork from the grandmother with the judge. Linda knows this judge to be very favorable toward adoption. We never saw or signed any documents.

Nori's birthday was sometime during that week, and he was going to turn ten. We hoped we'd meet him before his birthday, but the paperwork dragged on. One day, he was supposed to return home from school at the regular time of two-thirty, and the foster mother called Linda. She was all panicked because he hadn't showed up. She called the school, the school called the police, and finally he returned home around six P.M. He said he was at a friend's house, but the foster mother called to check his story and found out it wasn't true. He later admitted that a man and woman picked him up after school, taking him for a ride on the freeway. They bought him ice cream, took him to a house, asked him some questions, and then returned him. But he lost his clarinet during the kidnapping. Linda was very excited when she told me this story. She said that she was afraid we'd first see him by watching his kidnapping on the six o'clock news, but fortunately he returned home safely.

Then the judge called Linda with a ruling concerning Nori and us. The judge told Linda that we would be good candidates to be parents but there was an international concern tied to Nori. He recommended that we not go through with the adoption, that Nori's family had ties to the Japanese mafia and the birthfather had checked himself into a mental institution back east for his own protection. We were rather shocked by the whole outcome, and asked that our names be removed from any paperwork involving him. We never saw any documents. That's one of the things with Nori. Linda kept saying, "Well, don't you want to give up on this one?" I would tell her, "No, no, let's go ahead." She finally had to come up with that big long story. She was losing money on us.

Then the next thing was a five-year-old girl in Canada. Her name was Charlotte. Linda thought she was half Peruvian and half Japanese. Her mother was a psychiatrist, she had adopted her. But the mother was dying of leukemia and the doctors gave her six months to live. She was desperately looking for new parents. Linda said she had difficulty getting information because of the mother's work hours, and the time difference between eastern Canada and here made it more difficult. We requested a picture and it was supposed to be on its way, and we didn't get any more information. Then, the mother's leukemia went into remission.

I'd like to say at this point we were finally starting to wise up, but at the end of June she called us up about another one. This was a sibling group and they were in San Jose. They were half Japanese, one-quarter black, and one-quarter Caucasian. The mother had died of brain cancer and she'd grown up in a Japanese orphanage. She was half Japanese and half black. The father was recently injured in the Gulf War; he was paraplegic. He was half Japanese and half French Algerian. She'd talked to the father and he was really depressed.

If we wanted these kids we had to take custody of them right away, maybe even the next day. We said, "Can we see photos of them first?" Then she said twenty other couples had looked at the kids and turned them down and that's why the father was so depressed. Later that week I went over to her house and she brought us some photos. There was no way around it—the kids were black and that was it. Very cute kids, but there was no mix at all. And it was just, "Hurry, hurry, hurry, you've got to do this now." I said, "Forget it."

Then she announced that she passed her bar exam. We said, "Well, that's great, this makes things easy, you can do the paperwork for us." We had quite a few lunches, and this is when she talked more about her life. She said she'd adopted three children. Her oldest was about seventeen, she was a little bit estranged from the family, and she went to live with some relatives in Hawaii. Then she has a son; he's fifteen. He was also supposedly adopted from Japan, and he lives at home. The youngest son had developed mental problems because of his mother's drug and alcohol abuse, and eventually they had to commit him to a state mental hospital. He died about three or four years ago.

She talked a lot about other people volunteering to help out with her organization and that someone had donated a brand-new Xerox machine. She mentioned several times that she had this other client that was a very wealthy Japanese man, and he was trying to arrange for her to help buy a home because her real goal was to have this house where birth-mothers could live. I don't know if that actually ever happened, but at that time we just loved her so much we bought her a fax machine.

In September she had this new case with a sixteen-year-old

Japanese exchange student. She was due on December 27th, so again, you have to pick something, my birthday's on the 30th of December, so there's always this chance that the baby would be born on your birthday. There was this other hook. One of the birthmother's big interests was playing tennis, and Tom plays tennis. And the boyfriend was into sports cars, and of course Tom is into cars—make sure we have all the emotions in there. The father was a seventeen-year-old Caucasian. They both lived in Pasadena, went to the same high school. Her biggest concern about this one was the parents. She had to get the parents' permission because of him being a minor, and because she was an exchange student none of the sponsors or the school were supposed to know what was going on; they'd send her back to Japan if they found out she was pregnant.

We were supposed to meet them. We arranged to meet at the Buddhist temple in Little Tokyo where Tom's mom works. Tom's mother had a lot of questions about Linda because of all these stories and not having results. This was the time where she was actually gonna meet Linda. Tom was trying to be on Linda's side and trying to prove his mother wrong. He was trying to believe in Linda that much more. Someone had called the temple about two-thirty in the morning and spoke with one of the priests. The person said she was concerned because the girl was missing and the family was out checking all the hospitals and abortion clinics. They were really worried she'd gone to have an abortion. Thinking about it now, they weren't even supposed to know she was pregnant, but oh well. We hung around for several hours that day at the temple and finally went to lunch; she never showed, and that was it. Linda said usually these girls, they get scared, but they'll call back in a few days and everything will be fine. At the end of the week she said the police traced her to a flight back to Japan. The girl called from Tokyo to the host family and said she was broke, living in a boardinghouse, her family had disowned her and she wanted Linda to call us up and send her a ticket so she could fly back to the U.S.

Linda's like, "So, you want to get a ticket to send her back?" I remembered that Linda used to tell me that she'd had other cases where they would get tickets for the birthmothers to come back and they'd go to the airport and they wouldn't show up. She told me that story a couple of times and it really stuck in my mind. She starts asking me for money for the ticket, and that was the time I saw red flags run up. I said, "Wait a minute. They have socialized medicine in Japan. You make arrangements, you park her over there, you say you've got doctors' connections over there. This seems the thing to do."

She couldn't argue with that one. She was really directly asking for money. It was going to be pretty clear-cut that we were supposed to come up with this plane ticket. Anyway, they supposedly got her examined over there and they said she was suffering from toxemia, but she had to wait for an opening to get into a maternity hospital. At this point it was starting to be a joke. Linda called me at nine-thirty in the morning, told me that the birthmother in Japan had checked into a maternity home. They decided her health was at risk, so they induced labor. She called me back later on to say that

17

the little girl was born premature, she was two and a half pounds, she had labored breathing. She wanted to know what we were going to name the baby. And sticking with the "A" names, we went for Andrea. Some of the other information we got was that the baby was suffering from seizures, and sure enough, she had cerebral palsy.

First we got a lesson in club foot, then we got a lesson on cerebral palsy. We told her we were hesitant about adopting a child with special needs. She was really upset when she saw us backing out on this deal. She wasn't happy we weren't going to hook in on this next one.

Linda was beginning to have trouble with her eyesight. She was saying how she was really losing her vision. She couldn't see, she said there's holes in her vision. Sometimes she would see two noses on a face and no mouth. She could no longer read, and because of her vision loss she asked me to remove all references to her being an attorney on her flyers. [Elizabeth had been assisting Linda with graphic design work.] She was not sure she was going to be able to practice law because of her new disability. We heard that Linda had to go in for a CAT scan. There is a tumor on her pituitary gland that is progressively causing her vision to deteriorate. She told me about how scary the possibility of surgery was, that she didn't want to go through with it but this doctor said she might completely lose her vision. She was telling me all sorts of details about the surgery and she was going to have it done at Scripps in La Jolla. I talked to Linda's husband to see if they needed any assistance for the upcoming surgery. I said, "If she needs a ride, I can always take her." We even gave her a robe to wear during her recovery, but it was too long and I had to hem the thing up.

Linda's surgery went well. There had been a minimal amount of swelling and the recovery looked good. Linda had developed a rash and it was probably an allergic reaction, but she was still doing well. Then Linda's husband called. He said he thought we were about the closest couple with Linda that she'd ever had in her eighteen years of adoption work, that we were owed an explanation.

He proceeded to tell me that she never went in for surgery, she never had a tumor, she never passed the bar exam, she never even went to law school. He was distancing himself. He said he suspected something was wrong and he went down to San Diego, where he discovered there was no record of her in the hospital. He found her checked into a convalescent hospital and she was sitting with bandages on her head as though she'd had surgery. He said it took two hours of talking and calling the police and then he had her released from the convalescent hospital. She admitted to him that she hadn't had any tumors and no law degree. He brought her back home and he made her face the congregation in church that Sunday. Then she was supposedly admitted to a county mental hospital.

We were stunned. It took a couple of weeks to sink in. The whole thing was a fake—there were never any babies or birthmothers or anything else. I didn't want to believe it. Linda was always talking about the fact that she does these workshops on bereavement issues. Her thing was death; she's really wrapped up in that. She said her problem wasn't infertility, it was superfertility, and she's been pregnant so many times and the kids have died. Also, all of her couples are mixed-race couples, the children are always mixed-race, and the question is always are you going to accept a mixed-race child with multiple handicaps. My thought is that she's not full Japanese, she's something else. Maybe she was always an outcast and she has some physical disabilities and she feels like she will always be an outcast. She's like searching for that couple that will accept that and she will throw them the hardest test case she can. The baby is her, kind of.

I think she and her husband were very deeply involved in this thing together for many, many years. Maybe she was more active at the end there; maybe he got scared a few times and wished she'd quit. But on the other hand, I'm guessing she makes $30,000 or $40,000 a year sitting in the kitchen using the telephone. It was a heck of a way to learn a lesson, but it has opened my eyes. When people tell me things now, I don't accept it as fact anymore. I try and check things out as much as I can. I had a master work me over.

TOM AND ELIZABETH hired me at about this time. For the next year or so we contacted clinics, doctors, churches, and others in the Asian community, searching for an Asian or a partially Asian child to adopt. None of those efforts produced results, but there was more to come.

★　　★　　★

20

A birthmother called our lawyer and we went and met her that day. She was very close to my age and was from a rather well-off family in England. She had two children, both from previous marriages. We really hit it off with her. I was relieved to see that she was a little bit older and maybe didn't fit the typical birthmother profile, so that maybe we had a little more in common.

The birthfather had been with her for about six months, starting a little before the pregnancy until about halfway through. Then he left the area and caused her great financial hardship. He said he'd help support her and he didn't. He had made many different promises that he did not live up to. The last time she saw him he was getting on the Greyhound bus with some artwork to sell. He'd not had contact with her for several months.

The birthfather is Chippewa. We were quite aware of the Indian Child Welfare Act. We knew enough to know that this could be a problem, but we were still willing to enter into it.

With the Indian Child Welfare Act, it's like having three birthparents that have to agree to the adoption. You have the mother, you have the father, and you have the tribe, and they all have equal rights to say no. We made every effort in good faith to get their ruling on it before the child was born so that if they were going to say no we could back out before we got further involved in it. We had made up our minds if they said no that we were not going to pursue it. Everything was done at the tribe's own sweet pace and they were as vague as possible, making no answer one way or the other. I think they waited to respond until after the child was born because they wanted to have the birth certificate filled out, to be sure that the birthfather [a Chippewa] was named as the father. I heard that there's some belief that they don't claim the children until after they're born. They implied that the child was to be returned to his father, which I think is rather presumptuous on their part, considering the fact that he had not been responsible up to that point. In any event, they said the child had to remain with one of his natural parents, that there was no way they would ever allow adoption or even guardianship.

They made it very difficult on the birthmother, because they did not offer her any financial support beyond the Indian clinic, which in an area such as this are not easily accessible. And that's about it. Her choices were to give him up to a tribal social worker, or she could give him to the father—but the father wasn't around—or she could keep him. She was pretty well on her own. Because she was fairly strong-willed and she felt very upset by the situation, she chose to keep the child.

She had about $200 to her name and no place to live. She had a lot of debts and no car. Because she's English, she had absolutely no concept of why the laws in this country allowed another group to have so much power over what she sees to be her life. She got letters from her family and they could not understand how this unknown entity of a tribe, who was neither the mother nor the father, could stop the adoption from going through. I think once we got the word "no" from the tribe I accepted that pretty much as final then and there on the spot.

About five days after the child's born, the father showed

up. His presence was very stressing to the birthmother, and that's when she started talking about his being involved in AIM, the American Indian Movement—AIM is a militant group, borderline terrorists; let's leave it at that—and that he had knowledge of how to blow up cars with pipe bombs. He threatened her that he had a gun in the car and he was going to kill her and himself and all that kind of stuff.

He wanted to get back together with her again. She felt that after all she'd been through, and with the tribe saying no, she didn't want any part of this. He had been coming around, and she felt very unsafe alone at her apartment. So we told her that she and the baby could move in with us.

Originally we thought it might be a couple of months that she might live with us. It got even more indefinite after a couple of months. I felt a certain amount of affinity toward Patty. I just wrongly assumed that we could really be friends, and really be kind of close. I assigned certain characteristics to her because of her age that I found out weren't really there.

I was going to go out and save the world and I was going to help this gal get back on her feet, and I could see us doing great things and all. This is why I learned that I cannot fix other people's lives. Tom saw me digging us in deeper and deeper. I take full responsibility. I can only do that because our son is sitting here now and we're laughing about it.

There was a turning point in all of this when we took a trip up to northern California with a car club. Patty brought along her nine-year-old son and we spent the weekend. I was getting along very well with her son. She was having trouble with him at that point, and it started a jealousy. That's when things fell apart. It started to get kind of ugly. Every night when we came home there'd be another crisis and there'd be something that wasn't working and you'd plan to go out or something like that and she'd say, "No, I don't have any money, I can't do that." She'd be complaining about the baby's father; he was calling pretty much every day. And we weren't sure how honest she was being with us about that whole event and what was going on. Meanwhile, she was trying to get welfare, and the welfare system is difficult to get into.

We were really hoping for someone to come along for her. She was saying herself that she was really tired of being with just the baby and us, she wanted a man in her life. I made a license plate frame for our old car that we had given her and it said, "She'd rather be riding a Harley." And while visiting a friend's shop some guy saw that and came in and asked who the owner of the car was and they met and went out on a date and he really liked her and thought she was the best thing that had happened to him. He knew that she had a little boy and thought he was the greatest little boy and really liked him, and two months later they moved in together. She doesn't have it on her car anymore either. I think he took it off!

We took a little breather after she left us. I think it was good for all of us to have time away. But we have definitely stayed in touch with her and as per her wishes, we became her son's godparents. In England the godparent is equivalent to having the right of adoption, and she felt this was very important. She had other friends who she was closer to, but she felt it was very important that we be his godparents. We were very honored by it.

I still think the Indian Child Welfare Act has a valid place, but I feel that there need to be more guidelines. Once the tribe is contacted I feel that they need to respond in a timely manner, not just what's convenient for them. If someone in good faith contacts them, they have to in good faith reply to them. And I also think that there should be guidelines as to what percentage of tribal blood is required to be accepted into it. If the tribe had been more agreeable to everyone involved, they might have built some kind of cooperative setup where the baby could have a good, stable home and could have contact with members. Instead, what they've done is said, "Nope, I want it my way or not at all." And so they didn't give the baby anything.

We had made an offer that we felt a proper education of his heritage was very important, and that we understood that it was more than the occasional Saturday visit to the museum to show him that Indians used to live this way. They made no effort to even respond to that offer at all. They were ignoring that this kid's got a father who kind of drifts in and out and makes big plans and then disappears for weeks at a time. He has a mother who in fact doesn't want to hear the word "Indian" because of what they've done. And the family—us—who might have been able to set something up with them and really do something good for him, as far as living in the dominant culture, of which he is half, and his own native culture, instead he gets none of that. Everyone ends up losing.

After that it pretty much left us thinking that if the stork doesn't deliver the next child on our deck, we weren't going to be bothered. We were not going to even pursue anything too hard. If it was going to happen, it was going to happen, and we were going to wait till something dropped on our doorstep. We got a call about a Cambodian child and we met with the birthmother and found out that the birthfather had a history of violence. We said, "Thank you kindly, good-bye." Because of our last experience we had no desire to be involved with anyone who had any type of thing like that. Because I guess what I didn't finish in our other story was, the birthfather made an effort, right after Patty moved out, to track us down and ended up spending two days camped out at our post office box, waiting for someone to show up. Even though it was hard to say no to the Cambodian baby, we felt that it was better to be alive and be whole than to be put through that. A couple months ago I heard something on the news about some Cambodian gang, and a shoot-out, and they went in and murdered some family. I heard it and thought, I'm glad we passed on that.

We just relaxed and we were not in any hurry at all. Sometimes Tom felt depressed. He would really like to have an adoption story come true. A lot of people set an artificial deadline of, "Oh, you're going to turn thirty, you'd better get married" kind of thing. Somehow forty was a very sensitive age deadline for Tom. He thought that he should have a child by then. We had tried all different avenues and we'd tried all kinds of places and contacted hospitals, social gathering places, whatever, particularly in the Asian community. We were not getting any response. Tom said, "We're open to anything," and so that was the first time we threw the net much wider.

We got the call a day and a half later; it was about four-thirty on a Friday afternoon. I was looking forward to a big, nice, quiet, long weekend, and into the fire we went again. There was a little boy who was born the day before. He was Hispanic. We went to see him that evening. We looked at him through the window and he wiggled his little fingers and, you know, he looked pretty healthy to us. He just had a good look about him.

Everyone at the hospital was so helpful. They said, "Oh, we hope this works our for you." We were smiling and saying, "You have no idea." I really think my reaction was, Well, looks good, let's take it one step at a time—the AA approach to adoption. I felt, We'll see in the morning if he's still there and if the mother's available to sign paperwork. Because we had to make that decision; if she wasn't going to be able to sign paperwork and if it was going to turn into a harder situation, we weren't sure we were ready to go through with it.

Five months later the adoption is going well and things look like they're going to be finalized. My friends ask, "Is it done yet? Is it done yet?" I have to keep explaining the process to them, the amount of time people have to change their mind, and it is just something people who have not been through cannot understand. There seems to be the sentiment of, This is ridiculous, why are people able to go back and change their mind? I think almost anyone who's been through an adoption feels that way. If you've done the necessary paperwork why are there these lengthy waiting periods and why do people have the ability to go back and change their mind after the fact?

In our son's case, I think the decision to place him for adoption was made at birth. I believe for anyone to make a good decision they have to have some time to make it. But in most cases of business you don't get three-month windows, six-month windows, whatever, to make up your mind on some kind of decision. And even though I realize that this is a real, lifelong decision, many decisions we make are, and so I feel it should be a much shorter period of time. In fact, most people say when you make up your mind it's in a split second, it's in a moment. It doesn't take you two weeks to make up your mind.

We were talking about the adoption the other night. Tom looked at our son and he said, "We couldn't have done better if we'd tried on our own." I know they all say this, but now that I'm here on the other side of it, yeah, it was all worth it. At least it's got a nice, happy ending to it now.

Update

ELIZABETH AND TOM have moved to a more rural community to raise their son. They do not wish to try and adopt a second time.

Comment

ELIZABETH AND TOM were embarrassed as they recalled their stories about Linda's manipulation of them. "It all seems so obvious now," both they and their friends say, but none of them thought so at the time. Linda had been referred to them by one of the oldest and best adoption agencies in southern California, as a reputable person who had strong ties with the Asian community. Prior to that, she had worked for a high-profile adoption attorney. If agencies and attorneys can be so easily duped, how can preadoptive parents protect themselves from frauds and scams like those Elizabeth and Tom suffered through?

The uncomfortable truth is that there is no complete protection. There will always be con artists, and those who receive enjoyment from the pain of others; but there are actions everyone can take to limit the possibility of being taken advantage of to the degree that we saw here.

A consultation with an adoption attorney should have been the first step Elizabeth and Tom took to protect themselves. An adoption consultation is a meeting with an attorney lasting two or three hours in which adoptive parents are educated about how adoption really works, the choices they need to make, and the pitfalls they may encounter. Without this, a preadoptive couple is flying blind and making potentially disastrous decisions. Elizabeth refers to an adoption one of her colleagues was going through with an adoption attorney and says that she had the impression that "attorney adoptions" were somehow shady. In California, 85 percent of all adoptions are independent adoptions, or "attorney adoptions" as Elizabeth called them, monitored and tracked by the state. Only after a comprehensive home study is completed and the birthparent's rights are terminated will the court grant a finalization of the adoption.

After their consultation, Elizabeth and Tom should have hired an adoption attorney, one whose practice is comprised almost exclusively of adoptions. Attorneys in other legal specialties are the wrong choice for adoption. Several of Linda's comments and explanations about the various situations she and Tom encountered would have been seen immediately by an adoption attorney for the nonsense they were, and the "adoption" would have gone no further. For example, the idea that a judge would have called Linda with a ruling about Nori, the nine-year-old boy, and recommended that they not adopt him is laughable, and never occurs.

This is not to say that attorneys are infallible or offer a hundred percent protection. I, too, was taken in by Linda for a short time, while working with another client. In that case, because the verification of pregnancy never arrived and the birthmother was, conveniently, a migrant worker and could never be reached, the "adoption" stopped very quickly—but not before the adoptive couple had the joy of being "chosen" and the pain of seeing their "birthmother" disappear.

Adoption is a highly specialized field. For most people, it is one of the most important and expensive experiences in their lives. And yet those who would never consider buying or selling a house without a real estate agent are happy to try and adopt a child without a lawyer. Whatever else adoption is, it is a legal phenomenon. To attempt it on one's own is dangerous. Several of the most horrific adoption stories I've heard involved well-meaning adoptive parents trying to save money by not hiring a lawyer, or hiring them only after their problems had become too big to solve. Without experience and expertise, adoptive parents cannot maneuver themselves safely through this very complex series of events.

The experiences Elizabeth and Tom had with Linda should have been enough for any ten adoptive couples to endure, and it should have been their turn to finally get lucky. Instead, with their birthmother Patty, they came up against the formidable federal law known as the Indian Child Welfare Act. What ICWA says, in essence, is that if a child has enough Indian blood to qualify for membership in the tribe, then the tribe, and not the birthmother, should decide who adopts that child. In this case we saw the unfortunate consequences of this law—a birthmother was forced to keep a child she didn't want to raise. Luckily, she grew to love the child, but at the time she left the hospital she had no desire to keep or raise him.

One complaint this birthmother had against ICWA was that half of her child's heritage was ignored and dismissed as unimportant. The child was 50 percent English and 50 percent Native American. But under the provisions of ICWA the English half doesn't count. Once Patty was forbidden by the tribe to place her child with Elizabeth and Tom, ICWA offered her only two choices: to send the child into a situation she saw as detrimental to his well-being, or to keep a child she didn't want. The "option" of giving the child to the tribe was completely unacceptable to the birthmother. She knew the birthfather's reservation fairly well, and she knew he had four other children there whom he didn't live with or support. He had not supported her during the pregnancy, and she had no reason to believe her child would fare any better on the reservation than his other children. His rights were not being challenged or terminated by the tribe—only hers were disputed. Indeed, it was not even clear that he wanted the child; but the tribe had the right to place the boy with another tribal family if the birthfather didn't want to raise him.

Another problem with ICWA is that it is supposed to apply to children who "qualify for membership in the tribe." However, tribal membership criteria are generally unpublished and sometimes undefined, bringing that much more confusion and mystery to the definition of "Indian child" and to the determination of who exactly qualifies for membership in the tribe. ICWA is our only federal adoption law, and it was never intended to apply to independent adoptions. It was meant to stop the abuses of previous decades, when Indian children were taken, sometimes involuntarily, from their families by public agencies and adopted by Caucasian families. Its application to independent adoption has caused great heartache, animosity, and controversy. In California it also extends the amount of time a birthmother has to change her mind, because her consent may not be signed until clearances have come back from all the branches of the tribe she has named saying that they do not believe ICWA applies in her case.

The stories of the abuses of this law are legion. Children who are 1/32nd Indian have been ordered to be taken from adoptive homes and given to birthparents who have no current or past association with the tribe. The birthfamily may never have participated in tribal social, cultural, or political life, and may not even know the location of the reservation. The jurisdiction of the tribe extends until a child is eighteen years old; the child may be removed from an adoptive home at any age if it is found that the provisions of ICWA were ignored. Ten-year-old children have been removed from their families under ICWA's power.

There are serious efforts being made to amend ICWA so that it will not apply to independent adoption. The sooner this can be done, the better for adoption, adoptive parents, birthmothers, and the children for whom they seek a secure home. The selection of adoptive parents should always be up to the biological mother. No woman should ever be forced to decide between keeping a child she doesn't want and giving it to an uninterested birthfather or stranger.

2

A Grandmother's Tale

AMELIA

A birthgrandmother

"My grandchild is my right."

I'm not even sure why, but in September I suspected that my daughter was pregnant. I asked her and she told me no. I accepted that; I really didn't have a reason not to. A few months later I noticed that she was gaining weight. At that time Christy had just stopped riding a bicycle everywhere and had gotten a car. She said, "Now that I'm not riding my bike all the time I'm putting on weight." One acquaintance of our daughter gave birth living at home with her mother, and her mother never knew that she was pregnant. I was amazed; I couldn't imagine how that could happen. Now I know.

Christy had this strange habit during her pregnancy of chewing ice. The minute she would walk in the door she would head for the refrigerator and she would start getting ice cubes. From daylight to dark she chewed ice. One of my aunts noticed that she'd gained weight, then noticed the crunching ice and said, "Oh, your uncle had those same symptoms right before they diagnosed diabetes." Because I didn't want to believe she was pregnant anyway, I was sure she had diabetes.

The baby was born in March. Toward the end of January I said, "Christy, you know, if you are pregnant, at some point you've got to tell me. It isn't going to go away, and we have to deal with it whatever it is." She sat and looked down for a long time, and at that point I knew. She looked up with these tears in her eyes and she said, "Yeah, I am."

I said, "Why did you ever think that you could not tell me?" I know I'm a caretaker, and have been for my family. I tend to be strong; I tend to think I know what everybody should do to solve their problems. So that's my tendency. But for some reason, that day I was able to say, "What are you going to do about this; what are you going to do now?" I didn't jump in and try to tell her.

She said, "I've thought about it a lot and the reason I didn't tell you is that I was trying to handle it myself. For a long time you've been telling me that I'm twenty-three years old, it's my life, I'm not a child anymore, I need to figure out things for myself. That's what I was trying to do." Christy has had a lot of struggles in her teen years and her early adult years with drugs and with becoming independent. So I think sincerely in her heart she wanted to be able to handle it some way without coming to me and asking me to figure it out for her.

She said, "When I first went to the doctor I intended to

have an abortion. I thought I might do it without you ever knowing." She found out that her insurance did not include terminating a pregnancy. It included prenatal care and care for the baby and the mother afterward, but it didn't include terminating.

As soon as she knew that she wouldn't be able to have the abortion, she thought it through and talked to the birthfather, but she pretty much told him that she decided she should place the baby for adoption. Dennis, the birthfather, came into Christy's life about three years ago. I still remember the first time she told me that she'd met Dennis. She thought he was very kind; he listened to her and he talked to her. I know he's had his share of problems and difficulties in his life, too. Dennis is quite a bit older than Christy, about nine years. She and Dennis connected right away. It appears that his family was trying to get him to become independent and self-sufficient as well. He wasn't living with them, but he really didn't have anywhere to live. He would stay with people or friends for a while. I know that drugs have been a part of Dennis's life, but I don't know when.

Prior to this, Christy went through a drug rehab program. It was an inpatient program and she was a patient there for a little less than two months. At the time I didn't know what kind of drugs she was using. Since then she's told me, "Everything," and I'm quite sure that's true, including intravenous use. She ended up in the program because I was finally able to give her the choice of either going into an inpatient treatment program or leaving the house. It had gotten to the point that I just couldn't bear the pain of watching her destroy her life, and that's all that I knew to do.

She'd gone to Colorado after the rehab program to get away from her old environment of bad habits and bad friends, and when she came home her intentions were to do some good things and take some positive steps for herself. Coming home and immediately connecting with Dennis, who was at an extremely low point in his life, probably wasn't the best thing to happen. She was in a pretty vulnerable place herself. She drifted immediately back into the same patterns.

In the three years that Christy has been involved with Dennis he has been in jail at least three times, usually for one or two days, and then they let him out; it's for things like tickets he hasn't taken care of. He was arrested for driving Christy's car with a suspended license. This happened twice. I got the car out the first time. I said, "I will do this once, because I will give you the benefit of making a mistake, but I will not do it again." The car was impounded a second time. I didn't get the car out, and she lost the car. But she doesn't ever seem to reach her limit with him, and with the effects on her life as a result. And once again, I had the struggle of knowing I could go get the car out, and having to stand strong and say, "I'm not doing this a second time."

They got together when Christy turned twenty-one. Soon after that Dennis's parents retired. His mother developed cancer and was gone within two months, which threw Dennis immediately into an even deeper depression. When she died, of course my heart broke for him, and I gave him the money to fly to the funeral, and Christy went with him. When they came back Christy asked me if Dennis could sleep on our couch, "just for tonight." I regret saying yes. I couldn't get rid of this person. I mean, I can laugh about it now, but oh, it's been awful. I was living in an apartment at the time and I had a two-car garage. Christy asked me if Dennis could put a few of his things in my garage. It became this horrendous nightmare. Dennis and Christy pick up anything anybody wants to throw away. I hired a trash person to come and clean out my garage twice. I think I've spent $200 having his trash hauled away!

Christy decided to move in with a girlfriend, and was working little part-time jobs. I was happy that she was moving out, because she and Dennis were not easy to live with. At that time I was getting to the point of realizing, This is her life, she's not sixteen, I can't continue to always be there trying to figure it all out for her, she is an adult now and I've got to realize that. It wasn't long before I learned Dennis was staying with them. Not that he was contributing—I don't think he was—but he was there. They got kicked out of the place where they lived. Then they rented another place, and they got kicked out of that. Christy had nowhere else to go and she asked if she could come home. I said, "Yes, you can come home. Dennis cannot come with you. Dennis has to learn to stand on Dennis's own two feet." Not only could Dennis not live there, he wasn't even welcome to come there. I knew by then that he was using drugs and didn't know she was, but of course I knew that it was likely. But I work, and I'm not there during the day, and I found that pretty much whenever I wasn't there, he was there. Finally, once again we reached the limit. I said to her, "If you bring him here again, you must leave." It happened again, and that's when she left with him.

Christy and Dennis have been pretty good at finding people who will let them stay for a while. As far as I know there was never a time when they were in a shelter or anything like that or sleeping outside, but I don't know that for sure. My daughter on the street—my daughter! It's almost like she wouldn't let me help her. I offered her a home under certain conditions, and she couldn't abide by them. Just like with the drug rehab, I didn't know what else to do except to set a limit and stick to it. After that, they found a place, where they were staying until the baby came.

When Christy told me that she had decided to place the baby for adoption I asked her if she was sure—you know, all the normal questions: "Have you thought this through?" And she had very sound reasons as to why this was her decision. She had many friends who have kept babies and she's watched the difficulties for the mother as well as for the child. She's had friends who've delivered babies after they've taken drugs and she has seen how worried they've been about the effects on the baby, but then continuing to try and live the same lifestyle. They've either raised them living with their own mothers or are living with the fathers. Some eventually have gotten married, some haven't, but all are struggling. Christy commented at different times when friends of hers would be pregnant and planning to keep their babies that she would never do that.

I told her that I did think that that was a responsible decision but she needed to be very sure. I wasn't quite confident she could go through with it. Also, there was a little relief, because as much as I have looked forward to having grand-children, I didn't want to *raise* grandchildren.

I asked her if she had done anything about trying to arrange for an adoption. She said the nurses at the doctor's office where she had been going for prenatal care had told her that they would get some information for her. This was about two months before the baby was due. I thought that there was still plenty of time for all of that to happen. I was checking something in one of the catalogues of the local community college and found a Saturday seminar called "Adoption: A Life-time Decision." The description said that it was a one-day seminar that would deal with all aspects of adoption, from the birthmother, the adoptive parents, and the adoptees.

I asked my daughter if she would be interested in going. I said, "If it's still something that you're considering, it's very important that you be absolutely sure that you can make this decision and live with it, that you won't regret it and that you think through all aspects ahead of time." I told her that I would go with her if she would like me to, and she said yes, she would.

A couple weeks later it was time for the seminar, and she wasn't feeling very well. I trust intuition so much, and it was almost like I knew somehow, or there was this feeling that maybe this was something more than just not feeling well. I was struggling with what to do because there was this inner feeling that this was something to pay attention to. It was either that emotionally she didn't want to go—which was making me a little uneasy; maybe this wasn't something that she was totally committed to—or that on the other hand, maybe physically something really was going on. I didn't want her to miss the seminar, because I felt that it was very important. The seminar was only going to be four hours, so I thought, We'll go to the seminar; if you're still not feeling well, or feeling worse, then we'll call the doctor later in the afternoon.

There were more people there than I expected, all ages of people. Christy was the only person that was obviously pregnant. Later, as everyone was introducing themselves, we discovered it was truly a cross section of different people who would be in the adoption process. There were birthmothers, there were adoptive mothers and parents, there were adoptees, there were two couples who were considering adoption. I was certainly the only birthgrandmother.

The seminar got started. I was really hopeful going in, wanting Christy to understand all aspects of adoption. But I felt that the seminar was definitely one-sided. It was negative; it was depressing, I'm surprised it didn't really turn her off from considering that adoption would be the right thing to do for her baby. The adoptees' experiences seemed to reinforce what the leader was saying, which was that there was this horrible loss, and that even without being told that they were adopted that somehow they had felt this loss throughout their lives. I think that I blame the leader a little bit in that she didn't recognize or seem to acknowledge that there were some positive sides. She didn't ask any of the people who were there about any experiences to the contrary. They were, traditionally, the kinds of things we thought about adoptions coming from the period of time twenty or thirty years ago; that would have been late fifties through the early sixties. I think that at that time it wasn't something that was talked about. You either got married and kept your baby or you went off and had the baby, and the baby was adopted and nobody ever talked about it again.

I think the leader left those people in the audience with the feeling that that's exactly how things are today. There wasn't any discussion about a different approach to adoption—of an open adoption, what that might mean today compared to what the people who were speaking had been through. I was hoping my daughter would hear something about how adoptions are handled today and learn about them in a way that would help her to make a decision. I wasn't feeling too good at the end of this because I felt that anyone who was going to make that decision had not heard very much that would make it seem at all positive. Two couples who were there were planning to adopt. If I had been in their place I would have felt frightened of the whole experience of adoption after hearing the discussion that day. I would have felt hopeless if I had been them. I would have thought, How could I ever take this on and create a loving, nurturing experience for a child? if what they heard was the whole truth. That would have made me run.

The rest of the seminar didn't offer anything different. It was almost a validation that everyone was a victim—the mothers who'd been forced to give up their babies and had been searching for years, the young people who had been adopted and felt somehow this abandonment and had also been searching. I've been through lots of versions of self-help groups and believe they serve a very valuable purpose, certainly helping people sort through different problems in their lives and hearing the experiences of other people. But I think there's a danger as well. At different times I've felt that people who are involved get caught up in being the victim of whatever their situation is, whether it's a codependent, an alcoholic, a recovering addict, whether it's an adoptee or parents searching for children. There's a danger of having that become your identity, almost to the point where you stay that victim.

I'm a codependent with my daughter, I know that. If I let myself I can sink into feeling "Poor me," that I'm the victim of all these things that other people are doing and I have to pick up the pieces. I'm always rescuing everybody. Well, I don't have to be doing that. I'm doing it, but anytime that I don't want to do it anymore I have a choice not to do it. And it's the same way I feel about anyone—you either stay in it or you figure out what you need to do to make something different.

After the seminar we met an adoption attorney [Randi Barrow] who offered to sit outside with us for a while and answer some questions as to what were some options Christy had. We talked for at least an hour, sitting on the bench. I think we learned more about how adoptions are handled today than we learned in four hours in the seminar, where we dwelled on how adoptions were handled thirty years ago. Thankfully, we learned they are handled very different today.

Christy asked all the basic questions that somebody would

have the first time. She wanted to know, "How are parents selected?"; "How do you get in touch with them?"—all those questions. We learned that the birthmother has a choice in selecting the adoptive parents. People who are interested in adoption prepare resumes to introduce themselves. We saw some resumes of couples, and they had their pictures and each one told about themselves and each one was very special in its own way, explaining their reasons for wanting to adopt a baby.

I think it was a real eye-opener for us to begin to understand the process and to realize how many people are really so committed to being parents and have tried many different options—fertility treatments and different things—and have spent many years trying to have children of their own. Adoption is one of those options that probably gets left until everything else has been tried. So these people are really committed to wanting a family, they've spent years thinking about it and planning for it. That was kind of a relief for us, to recognize that these aren't people who just wandered in one day and said, "I think maybe I'd like to have a baby" and that maybe next week they might change their mind. We were relieved at how thoughtful and committed prospective parents were.

There was one resume that Christy read and as soon as she read it she said, "I just think they're the ones. It feels right." I don't know how you feel that from a picture and a letter, but it did feel right. The couple were contacted; they called back later and were excited and anxious to talk to Christy. Later, they all got on the phone and Ben, the husband, told Christy that they had been out to dinner and that they'd been spending the evening talking about how good it felt to be chosen, that after all their years of trying and feeling that nothing was going to work out for them, it was so exciting for someone to pick them. Nothing had been decided; it was just that they were feeling good that someone wanted to consider them.

We learned later that they'd been through years of trying to have a family and were involved in one adoption proceeding that didn't work out, where the birthmother had changed her mind. But they were still feeling excited that she wanted to meet them. Ben was going to be leaving the next day for Japan and so Marci, the wife, was going to meet Christy for lunch the following Tuesday, then when Ben got back the next weekend they were all going to go out to dinner.

That night after Christy talked with Ben and Marci, she left. The next morning I was on my way to go to the office; I had a lot of work to do. I was just getting ready to walk out the door—I look out the front window and Dennis is dropping Christy off across the street. She's getting out of the car looking terribly bedraggled—she's barefoot; she looks like she slept in her clothes—and she comes across the street crying. She comes up to the front door, and she says, "I'm scared—I think I'm in labor." My heart dropped. Like I said, there was something intuitive the day before that we needed to take care of this immediately.

I didn't know what to do; I didn't know who to call first. I called Marci to tell her that the young woman that she was going to have lunch with on Tuesday is on her way to the hospital. I said, "We're leaving now; I'll call you as soon as I know what's happening." She said, "I'll be there—I'll be there as quick as I can."

I was really sort of in a dilemma, because on the last visit to the doctor they told Christy her medical benefits had been canceled, or had run out. They had told her if any problems came up before she was able to get this straightened out, that she'd need to go to one of the county hospitals. I knew I didn't want her to go there, but I wasn't quite sure what else to do. I felt it was an emergency situation and I drove to Mercy Hospital—that's where she was born; that's where I had all my babies. They couldn't have been nicer. It's a Catholic hospital, and I guess the treatment there was everything you'd expect from a Catholic-run hospital. I felt sure that they would take care of us, because the nuns do that!

By the time we got there Christy was having some pretty strong pains. They took her in at the emergency room, took her up to delivery. They admitted her even though they knew she didn't have insurance. They said, "Don't worry about it, you can come back and take care of it, we can work it out."

I went up to the fourth floor, where they have the maternity patients, and she was already hooked up to a heart monitor. So I walked into the room listening to the baby's heartbeat. Christy was scared. They were trying to reach a doctor. In the meantime, the nurses examine her. The baby was breech; everything seemed to be OK. They wanted to try to keep her from delivering until a doctor could get there. As soon as he got there he examined her and decided they needed to do a cesarean.

Christy was scared, but she was handling it all pretty well.

The nurses and everyone were very kind to her. At that point they didn't realize it was going to be an adoption. And actually, nothing had been worked out so we didn't know what was happening either. The doors into the delivery room were all closed but immediately I heard this very, very strong crying voice. The baby was crying and crying and crying, and the nurses come in and say, "It's a girl, and she's doing fine, and everything went fine." She just kept crying and crying. It didn't take very long until they came out of the delivery room with the baby, and for as loud as she had been when she was born, the first time I saw her she was in her little incubator as peaceful as could be.

They brought her over to the window. She was all wrapped up in her little blanket; her big eyes were open. I know grand-mothers always see these beautiful babies, but she was really looking around like she was observing things. I thought: This innocent baby is looking around at things, she has to be won-dering, What is going on here? Where am I? Here is this innocent, peaceful little baby and there's so much turmoil and indecision going on around her, but she seemed totally un-aware, and totally peaceful and contented where she was. For the rest of the time I saw her in the hospital, I never saw her cry again.

It was such an emotional experience. I was concerned about my daughter, as any mother would be, and at the same time I'm wondering what Marci's reaction is going to be to all of this. I was there by myself—I'd barely had time to call anyone. I left a message for Christy's father. When he got to the hos-pital he saw me and said, "Well, why are we here? I got your message that you were at the hospital. Are we here for an orientation?" He had been to a bon voyage party for a friend, brunch or something that morning, so he was not real clear on where he was or why he was there. I said, "No, no, Bud. Do you want to see the baby?" He said, "What baby?" I thought, Christy's dad is about as aware as she is in a lot of ways.

He walked down to the nursery with me, and then I saw Marci and her parents arrive. They wanted to see Christy; she was still back in the delivery area. Here she was, not looking her very best, either when she got to the hospital and certainly not after having been through all that, and that's the first time they were able to meet. So all the plans of getting acquainted and getting to know each other and getting comfortable with each other went right out the window.

I can't imagine what Marci was thinking. If I think we were going through ups and downs on our end, it must have been very, very hard for her. Here's a couple who wanted a baby for years. Suddenly they made contact with someone and they're expecting they'll have time to get to know the birth-mother and that both sides will make a decision in this matter. Suddenly the baby's born, and we're saying, "Here's your baby!" I don't know how they were able to make the decision. I'm so grateful that they did.

I felt comfortable with them immediately. Her parents were wonderful people and they talked so lovingly about their whole family. They were very kind to Christy, very sensitive to the difficulties of making the decision. They seemed to understand where she was coming from, that it wasn't an easy thing for her, and that it wasn't an easy thing for us. We were very grateful for the opportunity to meet them, because the more information you have about where the baby's going and the people who will be her family, you begin to create a picture of what her life will be like. Marci brought Christy some flowers that she'd grown in her garden; they were just sweet people. We all left to go downstairs to get some coffee and to get acquainted. It was like we'd all known each other forever. They were just the kind of people that under different circumstances I would have loved to have had for friends.

I always say about my daughter-in-law that if I would have interviewed for a daughter-in-law, I would have chosen her. I feel the same way about Ben and Marci. If I would have interviewed for parents for my grandchild, knowing that it couldn't be my daughter, then I would have picked them. I feel like they're a gift. I don't even know how to explain how I feel about them. I feel like they're, in a way, extended family. I don't plan to be a part of their lives, and I don't try to be because I feel strongly that they deserve to be total parents, without any distraction at all. But I feel blessed that I know that they are the parents for my grandchild. I feel pride in knowing that they're the parents, because of the kind of people that they are.

Saying that doesn't take away anything from how I feel about my daughter, or that my first choice would have been that she was in a position to raise her child and that I would have her in my life on a regular, daily basis. But that couldn't be, and so given that, I think that Ben and Marci are just a blessing in our lives.

Christy had talked to Marci and asked if they had been able to decide on a name. Christy's intention was to name the baby whatever Marci and Ben had decided. But they hadn't had the chance to be together and to really talk about it. So Christy went ahead on the last day before she was to leave the hospital and named the baby Emily. But Ben and Marci decided to name the baby Christy, which is a special, special thing. I was very surprised they decided to do that. I'm sure adoptive parents have all sorts of anxieties and paranoia and lots of worries about taking on that responsibility, and with always that fear that someone could change their mind. I guess I thought they would want to get as far away from any connection or any reminder as they could, but they didn't. They said they had always talked about that name.

The whole sequence of events had to happen when it did. We didn't know it, but it had to happen when it did. I just think that somehow the whole sequence of events were meant to take place. They were meant to happen.

The baby was very healthy—she was seven pounds, twenty-one inches long—and initially we thought everything was perfect. She was sleeping and eating and being the perfect doll. On the second day I went to the hospital right after work. I stayed for a while with Christy, and then went down to the nursery. I probably got to spend an hour just holding her and rocking her. She was the sweetest little thing. About the time I was ready to leave, the nurses were changing shifts. One of them came over to me and was talking about her and said, "It's really too bad that your daughter isn't going to keep her. Does she really want to have her adopted?" I said, "Well, no, she doesn't want to, but she's decided she believes it's the best thing." She said, "What about you—can't you take care of the baby?" I said, "I can't. I work: I support myself. I'm single—I have to work. I don't know how I would take care of her." I didn't go into it with her but my feelings were, Of course there's some way you can do it, but is that the life this little girl deserves? Of course I can continue working, of course she can go to child care. I worked and my children were in child care, but it's different being raised by a working grandmother as compared to being raised by a mother. But I didn't go into that with the nurse.

We kept talking and finally she said, "Yes, it's really too bad about the drugs." I said, "What drugs?" She said, "Oh, you didn't know?" I said, "No, I don't know anything, what's going on?" She said, "You can't say anything because I'd lose my job if they found out that I told you." I said, "Wasn't anybody going to tell me?" She said, "Well, the baby tested positive for drugs." My heart just sank.

I didn't know if Christy knew this—I didn't know anything. It was late by then. I didn't confront Christy with it; I needed to sort it through. I didn't know what had been discussed with Marci, I didn't know how to discuss it with her, I didn't know what to do.

When I got there the next day Marci was in the nursery with the baby, and she was holding her and feeding her. So I went in and Marci told me that she knew about the drugs and I told her that I had just learned about it the night before. I didn't even know any details. I didn't know how severe it was, or what it meant, or anything. Marci told me she had found out the day before when they did the test and she talked with the pediatrician. I was there for a long time with Marci and her sisters. Finally they needed to go and Christy walked down to the nursery and we were all there.

Later, I went back with Christy and she started crying and said, "I felt very left out." She was saying she felt very alone and left out, that she'd been by herself that morning for a while, and then she walked down and saw us all there with the baby. Until that point I hadn't said anything about the drugs. I felt bad for how she felt, but I felt angry too. I said, "You know, right at this moment you're not the most important thing. What's the most important is the baby." I said, "Marci is very upset about the situation with the drugs. She has not known what to do and I needed to talk to her. It isn't that I forgot about you or I'm not caring what you're going through, but right now I'm angry with you. I'm angry that this little baby is in danger because of the choices you made. Right at this moment it doesn't matter to me what you're feeling. When I take you home tomorrow you're going to get my full attention, my full care and concern, and I'll be there for you one hundred percent. But we've got to get this baby's life settled, and you've got to understand that she's all that matters right now."

She told me that Marci had been in to see her that morning and that she was very angry. I said, "You have to understand, we all love you and care about what you're going through, but you're not the only one here. Every single person involved is feeling the effects of this—you, as the baby's mother; Marci, in trying to make this decision and deal with this without her husband; her parents and her sisters, who have hoped for her to have a baby because they all have their children and she's such a loving, giving aunt to all of them and they all know how much she wants a baby of her own. They're excited for her, and now they're dealing with that pain. I'm dealing with this after having thought I understood the situation based on what you had been telling me, and now I learn that it's something entirely different. You're just one of the players in all of this. And yes, you're feeling your own pain and agony, but so is every single person here, each in a different way."

Marci told me that she'd been on the phone all the day before talking to her lawyer, talking to the doctor, the pediatrician, talking with a treatment center that treats methamphetamine babies. I think her doing that says so much about Marci and her husband and their character. This is a very difficult situation at best. She's hit with this, but she didn't just turn and run. She took the time to try and research it and try to find out everything that she could about the condition. She talked a lot with the doctor about the levels that had shown up. At that point I think she had decided that after having learned as much as she could, she was willing to go ahead with it. But she was very angry with Christy, and rightfully so.

Christy had assured me, when she knew she was pregnant, that she hadn't been doing any kind of drugs, that she had been taking care of herself. She had, supposedly, not even been smoking cigarettes that much. As I said before, in the beginning she was planning on having an abortion. I think at the time that she finally faced the reality that she was going to be delivering this baby, that's when she stopped doing whatever it was she was doing. I don't think that she fully accepted that until very late.

I don't know anything about drugs, so I don't even know if I'm calling it the right name, but as far as I know, that's what they found, methamphetamines, and there was not a large amount found in the baby's system. The pediatrician had just been in to test her and he said that on that day it was very, very minor traces, and that all the baby's reflexes were good and that at least as far as seeing any symptoms from an examination, they didn't see anything. It was just through the blood test that they discovered it.

During Christy's experience, for each of the different people in her family, it was difficult in different ways. Each of us has a lot of emotions and a lot of feelings around it all. Throughout this, everyone was as understanding and supportive as each could be. Nobody ever really confronted her angrily or accused her—we didn't attack her. We let her know that it was disappointing; we let her know that there were problems much bigger than anything she had intended that were created because of the choices she made. Her brothers don't really understand, because they don't like the boyfriend. They think he's a bad influence in her life and they're angry that he's a part of creating situations and then he leaves, lets other people pick up the pieces, and then he shows up again. He showed up at the hospital, after the baby was born, in tears, feeling very sad and sorry that they're not going to be able to keep the baby.

The anger comes out in me because here's someone who's

thirty-two years old, he wants to be with her, but he can't take care of her and he doesn't do anything to move toward them being able to be together. His choices affect my daughter. As much as I don't like the things that have occurred in my daughter's life since she's been with him, if that is her choice to be with him, I can live with it. But I can't live with, or I don't want to live with, wondering if my daughter is homeless, I don't want to live with wondering if she's doing drugs. I don't like having to watch my first grandchild be born healthy and knowing that she won't be part of my life. I'm angry with him for that. I know the two of them together share this, but if they are going to be so irresponsible as to allow themselves to become pregnant, then it's ridiculous for him to even talk to her about wishing he could keep the baby and at the same time never looking for a job. If he wants to live that way that's his choice, but don't bring this little life into the world under those conditions. That's the part I'm angry about.

My grandchild is my right—I mean, that is my right. Christy's life is hers, it's her right, but choices that she makes and that she makes together with him do affect mine. I wasn't ever prepared to feel the way I felt, even when I talked to her about her decision to place the baby for adoption. I supported her decision and I fully believe it was the right decision given the circumstances. But the circumstances are what make me angry.

Since the baby was born Christy's been at home, but there hasn't been an agreement that this is a permanent arrangement. What we discussed was she would stay here until she was through recovering, which is just about up, and at that point she would need to decide if she was going to stay or go back and live with Dennis. But the conditions of living at home are still the same—you work and/or go to school and do something that is contributing to you becoming independent and self-sufficient. Since the baby's been born it's appeared to me that she hasn't been quite as tolerant of him or of the excuses he makes for things.

When the baby was about a month old Christy was arrested on a warrant for failure to appear on an earlier charge of being under the influence of drugs. She had a court date in March. At that time she was just out of the hospital from delivering the baby. She didn't tell anyone she was supposed to appear or that she'd been arrested, because it could have been taken care of, it could have been postponed, any number of things. But she didn't tell anybody. I think a lot of how she deals with life is, nothing she does is ever intentionally aimed at hurting. It's more like just living in the moment, she doesn't think ahead to the results or the effects. And somehow she hasn't been able to learn that not taking care of things responsibly doesn't mean that they go away—eventually they just get worse. Not telling me about the baby left us one day to do something about the adoption. She still thought she had time. So there's always this side of good intentions, and then there's the reality of what happens when you don't follow through with your good intentions.

My daughter, in spite of lots of difficulties and lots of bad choices for herself, has never wavered from the decision that it was the right choice to have her baby placed for adoption.

I'm so, so, so grateful that she has stuck with it. I believe that maybe for the first time ever, she absolutely had her head together when she made this decision. She had thought it through; she knew that it was the right thing for her baby. She felt that she was not able to give the baby the kind of home that she would want to. She made a comment that she and the birthfather were not able to take care of themselves, so how could they possibly take on a baby.

I'm not sure where that determination came from. This is the one time also that she was not only able to make a good decision, which personally I agree with, but I also felt that I didn't influence her in any way. For one time I was able to be supportive without controlling things; I haven't always been able to do that, but I think in this case I did. I never told her, "You have to do it." I never told her I wouldn't be there for her if she decided to keep the baby. I just tried to support her decision, and she stuck to it. She never wavered. The only thing she said to the contrary was, "I wish it were different. It isn't different, but I wish it were different."

During the hospital stay she had lots of social workers and people who talked with her, and she went to counseling after the birth of the baby. So she's had a lot of people making sure that she considered all sides. It was not an uninformed decision in any way. In fact, there were times when I was beginning to feel they were almost trying to talk her out of it. But she stayed very, very focused on her decision. She's had some friends who have said, "How could you do this?" She tells them all the positive reasons why she did this— because she could not provide the environment she wished for her child. Regardless of what she has provided for herself, she did not want that for her child. She was able to reach down and find the strength and the wisdom to follow through with it.

We talk about the baby all the time, and so on the other side of it is there's just this wonderful joy and peace, knowing the adoptive parents are wonderful people. They're so generous in sharing the pictures and of just letting us know that they love her, and that their family, which is a large family, loves her and that they're feeling so grateful to have her in their life. I feel a loss, but I also feel a gratefulness that she's in their life. Thanks to them, it hasn't been a total loss. They're not in our presence, but they're in our hearts. We think about them, and love them and care about them. I cry a lot during all this, but it isn't from sadness, it's just from the emotions of the whole experience. I think it's very comforting and reassuring to think of her and know where she is and the family that she's with.

There's pain and loss that you feel as a birthgrandmother. There is most definitely sadness. It isn't sadness that things worked out the way they did, it's sadness that our lives were at a place that creates a situation where this was the best choice, that my daughter wasn't secure enough in her life at the time that she was giving birth that she could raise her child and provide a stable environment. I feel a sadness for my daughter—I'm sorry for her that she had to go through that. It isn't an experience that any mother would want her daughter to go through ever. But I'm proud of her for having made a good decision.

My daughter keeps the pictures of the baby in her room, and sometimes I just walk by and look at them all and I just go away smiling. I mean, how could you not? I think if it got to a time when little Christy naturally had a curiosity and wanted to make contact, that would be wonderful. But I think I want her to have all the security and stability that she needs in those early years, and I wouldn't want to confuse that in any way. I want Ben and Marci to feel safe. Christy doesn't talk about the baby every day now. The last time I heard her bring up the baby was when we were coming back from her recent experience in jail, that having been through that she again is reminded how much better the baby is being with them than having been with her. She knows she doesn't have her life together. She knows she's still not behaving responsibly and she's still able to see the benefit in all this, that the baby's not experiencing any of this in any way or being affected by it. She always related it to that.

The only time I've seen her express real sorrow and real regret or remorse has been in terms of how sorry she is that the baby was ever in danger. She said that she's looking at it now and having had the baby and having things turn out the way they did, she's very grateful fate worked the way it did and she wasn't able to have the abortion. I think my view of abortion has probably been complicated or clouded by this experience. I was very sure in how I felt about it, that it was a mother's right to choose, and certainly not that it should be taken lightly but that there were situations where that was necessary. I still think it has a place, perhaps, among the different options, but it would be much, much harder to make that decision after having been through this. Christy feels differently about abortion after having little Christy and knowing Ben and Marci.

Out of this comes one of the proudest times of how I feel about my daughter. I've been very frustrated and unable to help her in terms of coming to grips with her own life and changing her behavior so that there are more positive results for herself. I haven't been proud of a lot of the things she's done or been involved with, but I'm most proud at this point of what she's done in terms of her daughter. I don't know what it will take for her to change the direction for herself, but I still think there's a chance she can do it. Right now I think my biggest decision is deciding whether or not to have my own life affected negatively by the people she chooses to have in hers. That's my big dilemma right now, but I will make it.

Update

DENNIS'S FATHER DIED within six months of the baby's birth, and he inherited a considerable sum of money. He and Christy moved to a small town in rural California, near his relatives, to begin a new life together. Christy gave birth to another daughter two and a half years later.

Comment

BIRTHFAMILY MEMBERS ARE affected for a lifetime by a birthmother's decision. While their influence on the birthmother is powerful, they have no legal rights of their own; ultimately, they must accommodate themselves to her choices. Many people are surprised by the fact that a birthmother's age in no way affects her ability to place her child for adoption. If Christy had been twelve years old it would have been her absolute right to place her child as she wished.

When a planned adoption goes awry it is most often a result of the influence of a family member, especially the birthmother's mother. If she is against the adoption it is less likely that there will be a successful placement. The birthmother's final decision is almost never affected by the desires of the adoptive family, no matter how long they've worked together toward adoption, no matter how much the birthmother knows she will hurt or disappoint them. But it is affected deeply by her mother's opinion.

Amelia was fortunate, because she supported her daughter's decision and was pleased with her choice of adoptive parents, but none of the decisions were hers to make. Amelia had a strong influence on Christy, but it was not stronger than her daughter's desire to take drugs or her need to remain involved with the birthfather. Her daughter's choice, which gave Amelia such pride because of its selflessness and maturity, also caused her the loss of her granddaughter. And we must remember that although birthgrandparents have no legal rights in adoption, they have many of the feelings of all grandparents. I would not advocate for any decision-making power to be taken away from the birthmother, but I would encourage adoptive families to acknowledge that the adoption affects an entire family, and to extend their generosity accordingly, through pictures, letters, or calls.

Everyone from the family members, to the adoptive parents, to the social worker, to the birthfather want to know at some point in every adoption how they can control a particular aspect of the birthmother's behavior. But control with a capital "C" has little meaning in adoption. The more control adoptive parents, or any of those named above, try to exert over a birthmother, the riskier the adoption becomes; birthmothers, like most of us, resent other people's trying to manipulate their lives, and resist those efforts. I am not referring to the planning and the arrangements that are involved in every adoption, but rather to questions like, "Can we ask the birthmother to stop smoking during the rest of her pregnancy?" or "Could we ask the doctor to induce the birth early?"

For all her concern and love, Amelia was unable to control her daughter. Christy was unable or unwilling to control her drug use during the pregnancy, and neither birthparent could exert the self-control or discipline necessary to create a financially secure and stable environment that would have allowed them to raise their child. The adoptive family could not control which birthmother would choose them, or when, or when the baby would be born, or its sex or health. This lack of control was most vividly evidenced by the issue of drugs.

Christy had been in rehab before she met the birthfather, who had his own history of drug use. Most important, the baby tested positive for methamphetamine, also known as speed. No adoptive parents ever walk into my office and say, "We want to adopt a drug-exposed child," and indeed a few have walked away from a child they were planning to adopt who tested positive for drug exposure at birth. A seasoned health practitioner once said to me, "You have to give up the idea that you can ever know what a birthmother did while she was pregnant, and what effect, if any, her drug use will have on her baby."

Similar opinions are reflected in the scientific literature and in anecdotal stories. Prenatal drug use seems to affect some children some of the time, and no one can predict who or how. Adoptive parents have to make some of their hardest choices in this area and to be extremely clear about their boundaries. If they choose to adopt a child who has been exposed to drugs, they must first differentiate between those drugs—marijuana use and cocaine use during pregnancy are not going to carry the same risks. They must then be prepared for everything from comforting a child through withdrawal symptoms to simply watching for problems that may never appear.

When adoptive parents are investigating the effects of drugs in utero they are almost always surprised to hear a statement made to me by a researcher on this topic: "One of the worst drugs a woman can use during her pregnancy is alcohol." We have no real way of knowing if a birthmother drank during her pregnancy, and must go on what she tells us. Testing is limited because of the short period of time alcohol stays in the system in a measurable amount. And even if we know what the birthmother was doing, and when, we can't be sure if it will have an effect on *this* baby.

Marci did exactly the right thing when the baby's drug screen came back positive: She didn't flee in panic, but rather educated herself by speaking to medical practitioners, who see such children at birth and as they grow. Nor did she pretend to the birthmother that she didn't know or wasn't mad.

Little Christy has turned out to be an exceptionally bright and beautiful child, with no signs of impairment. Not surprisingly, when a child tests positive for drug exposure, most adoptive parents choose not to share this information with their families. They fear that the information will stigmatize the child, and that occasionally negative or painful, but *normal*, behaviors and emotions will be deemed to be the "lifelong legacy" of prenatal drug or alcohol use.

The idea of a negative and lifelong legacy extends not only to drugs and alcohol, but to adoption itself. The message at the seminar Amelia and Christy attended was, all too typically, that adoption is like a disease. For it has been made into a pathological issue by some members of the adoption community. The seminar leader referred to adoptees as "missing in action" and "prisoners of war." At one point the speaker held her hand a foot or so away from her abdomen and said, in effect, that when you're adopted it is as though you hear and see everything through this filter—adoption—and nothing is the same for you as it is for other people. To characterize adoption this way is inaccurate and unjust; it does damage not only to those involved in a particular case, but to the entire field. It casts a shadow over hopeful adoptive parents who are being told, in effect, that adoption is a losing proposition and that the adoptee is, and always will be, damaged goods. It is confirmation from an authority figure that birthmothers and adoptees are wounded by adoption and will stay wounded for life. Hard to ignore is the coincidence that those who declare adoption a lifelong "problem" for all involved have also created a huge market of people who now need to "fix" that problem, people who must seek and pay for the advice of those who condemned them to this "lifelong legacy" in the first place.

On the farthest edge of this negative view of adoption are the groups who advocate for the abolition of adoption. They see adoption as a permanent answer to what is only a temporary problem, one that the state should be required to solve by offering financial assistance. They ignore the reality that adoption is the wholehearted choice of millions of Americans. Problems arise when groups like these zealously pursue legislative changes that have little to do with current adoption practice or the attitudes and needs of the majority of birthmothers, adoptive parents, and adoptees. An institution can't be repaired with the help of those whose goal is to destroy it. These people add to the confusion already surrounding adoption, and pull resources away from the reform that it needs so badly.

Amelia and Christy went to their adoption seminar with a desire to learn and to be helped. What they came away with was a feeling that adoption, if it was as the speaker claimed, was a horrible thing. Fortunately, within twenty-four hours, Amelia and Christy were able to have an adoption experience of their own, one quite different from the one that had been portrayed to them as the norm.

3

The Phantom Father

COLLEEN

A birthmother

"I want my baby to know that he is mine, that I had him, that I still love him, and that I will always love him."

Me and a friend went into town to a football game. After the game my friend took off with some of her friends and I went down to the beach to find her. I went over to the rest rooms and when I came out, these two guys grabbed me and . . . well, that's what happened. They just left me there; I didn't move, I didn't tell anybody. I found my girlfriend and we came home. I felt like a lot of people wouldn't believe me because there was no evidence. I felt like there was nothing to prove it.

A couple days later I told my girlfriend. We kept it a secret. She knew I was telling the truth because she knew how upset I was, but she didn't know what to do about it. I was afraid people would think I was lying. That's just the way it is, you know? Hardly anybody knows about other girls in the town who've been raped. It's something a little town doesn't think can happen.

It would have been ten times as hard if it would have been my first experience. I would have died. I didn't have a boyfriend at the time. I got engaged to Ronnie two months after it happened. When he asked me to marry him, I told him. I never really think about the rape; it's just a mental block. That's one thing that I always do—really hard things, I never think about. And I never will. They're just, like, gone.

I knew right away I was pregnant. That's how my whole pregnancy has been. I have known everything that was going to happen. I knew when the baby was going to be born, I knew it was a boy, I knew it was going to be healthy. It was almost two months later that I finally told my mom. I knew she was going to find out sooner or later—I needed to go to the doctor and get medical treatment for the baby. I wrote her a note and put it on her bed. I can't remember exactly what I said, I just told her that I was raped and that I was pregnant. I was so afraid of what my parents would say that I just couldn't tell them face-to-face. The next morning my mom came into my bedroom and told me not to go to school, that we needed to talk.

She was very understanding. That helped a lot, because I didn't feel like I was in trouble for it, which is something I think all rape victims go through. They think everybody's going to be mad at them because of what happened; they think it's their fault. I felt like I shouldn't have gone down there. I don't ever go to that part of the beach by myself, I never do. We talked about what happened, who knew about it, and the way I was feeling. She told me that it wasn't my fault, that I had nothing to be ashamed of. She supported me in every way she could.

I knew that there was no way I could ever get an abortion. My mom brought it up as an option. She told me that I shouldn't feel bad about it because of what happened. But she is totally against it, and so am I. There's no way I could kill a baby. Like in my situation, I don't care what happened, that's still a little baby—that's murder. I wanted the baby because he's mine, but I never really focused my mind on keeping it. I thought I would always look at the baby and think about what happened.

When I found out a short time later that my sister Bridget was pregnant too, and was going to give her baby up for adoption, it hurt me really bad. I didn't feel it was right because hers was out of love and mine wasn't—I did not want to have sex. I never condemned her for it, I just didn't think it was right because that baby would have had everything, it would never have went without. When Bridget told me about her adoption she told me not to tell my parents. So here I am stuck with this enormous secret along with my own problem. I was shattered. I had to keep it from my parents for the longest time; I really resented that.

Bridget didn't really say anything about my pregnancy. When I'd go over to the store where she worked we'd always joke around—"You're fatter than I am," little things like that. But we never really talked about it. We talked about hers all the time but never about mine. I don't know why. I think she felt bad for me because of what happened. Maybe she tried to spare me bringing it back up.

My mom knew Bridget was pregnant, but Bridget didn't tell her about the adoption until a week before she went to Los Angeles to give birth. She was afraid my mom and dad would be disappointed because she was giving it up. They were so psyched for that baby; it was such a letdown to find out she wasn't going to keep it. My mom felt really bad, like it was her fault, that she was no good, that she had done everything wrong. I heard this every day—you know, "I can't believe Bridget's giving the baby up," and on and on and on. I was feeling really guilty because I was giving mine up too. I felt like, Does my mom feel this way about me too? She always told me she loved the baby. It wasn't like she loved mine any less that Bridget's. It's just that it was my decision and I had made it from the beginning.

When I told the doctor what had happened, about the rape and everything, he never really had a response. He never talked to me about the adoption. He just told me that it was a closed adoption and that I could never know the parents. He said when the baby's born I'll spend time in the hospital with it, and then the parents will come and get it. And he said, "You'll get pictures."

I was very hurt, because I didn't want it that way. I wanted to meet the parents. I wanted to see the parents, to know what they were like. I wanted to be able to keep in contact with them. I had read a book about it, *To Kira, With Love*. It's about a girl who gave her baby up for adoption. She got to meet the parents. They called her while she was in the hospital to see how she was doing. That's the way I wanted my adoption to be. She got pictures all the time, and she got letters from them.

I felt like the couple was not going to tell my baby that he was adopted, that they were not going to let him come find me. It felt like I would never see him again. I didn't want that, because I want my baby to know that he is mine, that I had him, that I still love him, and that I will always love him.

At first I trusted the doctor. I just wanted it all to be taken care of, I wanted it to be over with. I didn't want to have to deal with it. He's been my doctor ever since I can remember. I felt obligated to let him do it, and I felt comfortable because I thought he would not let my baby go to some bad people. I had been having so many dreams about the baby. One night I had a dream that I had a baby and they took me out of the room afterward, they didn't let me see the baby. When I got back into the room, the baby was gone. I started screaming, "I want to see my baby! I want to see my baby!" That's the way I felt about the way the doctor was handling it. I realized that if he would have ended up taking care of it, I would never see my baby again.

My sister went to California to have her baby and give it to the new parents. The doctors there thought that something drastic was wrong with it, and that it was going to cost a lot of money. So she flew back up here to have the baby because she had insurance in our state. My doctor came in to see her the night she flew back, even though she did not let him take care of the adoption. We were all sitting outside her room at the hospital. All of a sudden his voice starts getting louder and louder. She was the only one in the room—he wouldn't let anyone else in. She was really scared.

My mom went into the room right away. My dad just kind of moseyed along. He really didn't want to go in there, because he was gonna deck him. When the doctor would not quit yelling at my sister, my dad went in. She was sitting there with all these monitors hooked up to her, having a non-stress test to check the baby's heartbeat. She's having contractions, she's in labor, and he's saying, "There is another lady in here that needs to use that." It was like, "Hurry up!" The nurse turned around and said, "She can wait."

He said there was nothing wrong with the baby based on an ultrasound that he only walked into the room every once in a while for. I'm thinking, How can he treat her like this and treat me any different? How can he sit there and not resent me because I'm her sister? I decided that I wasn't going to see him anymore, but I didn't know what I was going to do, because I had never had another doctor in my life. My sister told her lawyer about me, that I was planning to put my baby up for adoption, and explained the situation that was going on with the doctor. I liked what I heard about independent adoption a lot better than what I had been going through. They were all my decisions, not somebody else's.

I don't really think I felt anything while I waited for the new couple's call. I think I was just in a daze, but I was excited in a way because I was going to meet them, I was going to talk to them. When I talked to them I felt it was right. I felt like they had known me forever. They were friendly and open-minded about everything. They had a lot of interests that I did, like being outdoors and traveling. They were just neat people. I feel like they didn't really care about the rape, because if they had, they wouldn't have called. I didn't want them to feel hatred toward the baby because of it or not love him as much as they're supposed to.

That night I didn't have any nightmares for the first time in months.

Update

COLLEEN HAS MARRIED and is the mother of a son. She keeps in touch with the adoptive family. Four years after giving birth, Colleen informed the adoptive family that she had been one month pregnant at the time of the rape. She said her parents "would have killed me" if they knew she was sexually active at the age of fifteen, and so she used the rape as the excuse for the pregnancy. The birthfather had been aware of the situation from the beginning. Now that he was preparing to marry someone else, both he and Colleen wanted to settle the birthfather issues with the adoptive family. Shortly after that his rights were formally terminated by the court.

Comment

EVEN A GREAT girl like Colleen will lie to protect her interests. In this case, she lied about an issue that terrifies adoptive parents, one that has burned the names "Baby Jessica" and "Baby Richard" into people's hearts—the identity of the birthfather. It was fortunate for the adoptive parents in this case that the birthfather had always known the truth about the conception and adoption and was cooperative in terminating his rights. It could just as easily have been a disaster.

In any adoption, the potential exists for deception on many important issues: drug and alcohol use during the pregnancy, sincerity about actually placing the child, and correctly naming the birthfather. No matter how often the importance of the truth is stressed, a lie will be told if it serves a birthmother's needs or calms her fears. Birthmothers don't want to reveal information about which they are ashamed, or that they perceive as threatening to the success of the adoption. It is hard to be too critical of a fifteen-year-old girl who is viciously attacked by rapists. And yet, Colleen's actions in misleading everyone about the birthfather could have caused terrible damage to the adoptive parents and the child, no matter how innocent her intentions.

Because a woman carries and gives birth to the child, thus assuming more responsibility and physical risk, the law grants her greater rights than the birthfather, unless she is married. If a birthmother is married, and her husband is the biological father of the child, her husband must consent to the adoption in almost all cases. If he does not, the adoption cannot occur, even if she consents. Most birthfathers are boyfriends, and generally speaking, they have two rights: the right to know that an adoption is being planned, and an opportunity to challenge the adoption in court. But the real or complete names of many birthfathers are unknown. Sometimes birthmothers have had sex with more than one man during the time in which they have become pregnant and the birthfather may be one of two or more men. We may never know their names, or, if we do, we may be unable to find them and give them the notice the law demands they receive. When an adoptive family does not know the identity of the birthfather it gives rise to fears that a man might come forward in the future claiming he did not receive notice and wants his day in court, even if all legal procedures were followed and his rights were properly terminated. It must also be remembered when we meet a birthmother that there is no proof that the man she names as the birthfather—even if that man backs up her claim—actually *is* the birthfather. We have only the birthmother's or the birthfather's word.

In light of the problems caused by not naming or by misnaming a birthfather, more than half the states have created birthfather registries in the last ten years. Under a registry system it is the birthfather who has the primary responsibility of protecting his rights. Most registries require a birthfather to register and thereby claim parental rights either during the pregnancy or shortly after birth, usually within thirty days. His registration guarantees his right to have his challenge of an adoption considered. If he does nothing, the adoption can proceed without notice to him. This protects birthfathers who have demonstrated a commitment to the responsibilities of parenthood, and gives no rights to those who do not.

The rationale behind this kind of law is that if a man is having intercourse with a woman, he should anticipate pregnancy as a natural possible outcome of that action. If he wants to preserve any rights he may have as a father, he must take action or lose his parental rights as they relate to an adoption. More rights are given to the men, who may be the fathers of these children, as the growing birthfathers' movement has been clamoring for, but it has coupled those rights with responsibilities. The duty is taken off the birthmother and the adoptive parents to identify and find the birthfather, which is often a difficult and sometimes impossible task. This can eliminate many expensive and sometimes heartbreaking court cases. It also discourages the birthfather who has no real desire to raise the child, but is challenging or stalling the adoption to get back at a birthmother for some reason, or simply to save face with his family or friends.

The fact that there are no interviews with birthfathers in this book is a reflection of their infrequent involvement in the adoption process. I meet a few each year who are involved with the birthmother and cooperate during the adoption process. But the typical adoption involves a birthfather whose first question is "How do you know it's mine?" after which he promptly disappears or becomes uncooperative. "You can do what you want, but I'm not signing anything" is a common birthfather refrain. As of this writing, California has no birthfather registry, and no legislation pending that would create one. It does provide mechanisms by which a birthfather's rights may be terminated, even those we cannot name or locate. But if a birthmother has lied in naming the birthfather, and he brings an action to establish his paternity, the adoptive parents can be faced with legal bills ranging from $30,000 to $250,000 to fight the case.

The birthmother, the birthfather, and the child are all given free, court-appointed lawyers. During the trial the child remains with the adoptive parents as they prepare themselves for the possibility of losing their child, even if they have done everything correctly under the law. Once again, we ask the child and the adoptive parents to put their interests in a position secondary to those of the birthparents, even ones who have lied or shown disinterest. Nationwide, only 1 percent of birthfathers actually challenge adoptions; but the more egregious examples of those cases, like Baby Richard, prevent some couples from even considering adoption. Without an affirmative duty on the part of the birthfathers, like those demanded by birthfather registries, the potential for problems remains.

Adoption demands and deserves certainty. The laws of most states clearly distinguish between a boyfriend and a husband, giving them very different rights, but are then often modified by case law, leaving even the experts uncertain as to the possible outcome of any given case. A change is necessary to bring about the security that adoptive parents and birthmothers need to proceed with the placement of a child. In Colleen's case, the birthfather would have automatically lost his rights by not coming forward when he knew of the pregnancy. There is no one way to deal with birthfathers' rights that will satisfy everyone or that is completely safe for adoptive parents; the facts of most adoptions contain inherent uncertainties. But the birthfather registries created by half our states strike a balance between the interests of the child, the birthparents, and the adoptive parents. They are fair and allow for speedy resolution, and serve as effective models for those states that have yet to confront this difficult problem.

4

"Where's Mommy?"

PAUL AND MARC

Adoptive parents

"I think that people would be surprised how much our family looks like their family."

Marc: We met at university as undergraduates. Paul is a director and I am an actor, and he was directing *Romeo and Juliet*. I did not get cast as Romeo, but I figured I had to pay my dues since I was only a freshman. He cast me as Romeo's little-known friend Balthasar, who only has a couple of lines. We became friends then, and the next year we worked together again, and that's when we started going out with each other. That was sixteen years ago.

The whole campus was pretty open-minded. And especially because we were in the theater, hanging out with the theater crowd, we were very open about our relationship. I come from a family of seven children, and came out to them over the course of about two years when I was an undergraduate, but in the context of my relationship with Paul. My family knew Paul, which I think helped tremendously. When I had dinner with my mother and came out to her, I was nineteen years old and I sat down and I was telling her that I was gay, and that Paul was the person I was going to spend the rest of my life with, and it must have sounded so naive, it was so much to handle at once. But sixteen years later, it's true.

So, by the time I graduated they all knew about us, and knew that I was gay. My family and my mother are very liberal, sort of accepting people. It was never a question for me that they would be anything but accepting and loving, and they were and have been. I think for them it helped tremendously that it wasn't a sort of abstract kind of life that they couldn't really know about and didn't understand, it was about this man that they all knew and loved very much. That made it all very easy for them to deal with, and Paul has been a part of the family since that time.

Paul: I think a lot of parents fear the stereotypes about gay life—that you're going to be lonely, that you're just going to go from partner to partner to partner, and that essentially you're doomed to a very lonely life. I was more terrified of coming out to my parents than anything in the world, and was not as courageous as Marc, or as quick as Marc. In fact, I did not tell my parents about our relationship until 1991. It was the fiftieth anniversary of Pearl Harbor Day that I told my parents that I was gay, and that Marc and I were a couple.

My mother in particular had made it very clear that if any of her children had news like that, it would not be news that would be welcome. So I just lived in terror of them knowing. Finally, I began to talk to my siblings one at a time about a year before I talked to my parents, maybe a couple of years before, and kind of worked my way up to telling my folks.

The first thing they did was reassure me that they didn't love me any less; that was the very first thing they said. They were not as immediately and fully accepting as Marc's family, but they've gone on a journey, they've struggled. But some of the most beautiful moments in our relationship were this past weekend having our son Jamie with them. They could not have been more loving or doting grandparents. They could not have been more accepting of the fact that both of us are Jamie's parents, and more complimentary about the parents we are, and the parents we're going to be. When I think how afraid I was and just what a journey it's been for me and them . . . We just had a family reunion where all of us were together for the first time in maybe four years, and Jamie was the highlight of the family reunion.

Marc: One of the most remarkable things of this past weekend at Paul's parents was Paul's father sitting us both down and really grilling us, asking us hard questions about what church we were going to raise Jamie in, and how that was so important. I was just amazed that here we were having a conversation with him where he could not have been treating us with more respect as a couple than to have this conversation, and ask us these really, really important questions about his grandson. It was beautiful.

When we met Jamie's birthmother one of the first things she asked us was, "Look, you guys are two white guys, and this baby is going to be very racially diverse. He is three-eighths African-American, a quarter Latino, a quarter Italian, one-sixteenth English, and one-sixteenth Sioux Indian. So, I just want to know what you're going to do to make sure he's connected to his heritage."

We said, "Well, this is what we do for a living, we do Foundation Theater, and this is what our goals are, and the kind of work we do." Foundation is a theater company. It's a consensus-run ensemble of theater artists, actors, directors, designers, administrators, and production people that was founded in 1986 by Paul and a woman who is an extraordinary playwright. The Foundation ensemble, which is right now seventeen people, which governs the company and actually does the work, is a very culturally, racially diverse group of people. We have made it our life's work to bridge different cultures and different experiences with theater. And Jamie, our son, is going to be raised within that environment, of just celebrating people's differences.

What we did in the first five years of Foundation's life is we traveled around the country and settled in mostly very rural, very small communities, sometimes as little as 150 to 200 people. We would do plays with the people who lived in those communities and our company, usually adaptations of classics, classic texts that were adapted to be about the community that we were living and working in. We would be there for three to four months, and then move on to a new place.

We just finished a series of residencies with communities that all begin with the letters "B. H.," like Beverly Hills, Baldwin Hills, and Boyle Heights. After a series of residencies like that we do "bridge" shows, where we hire folks from the past communities and bring them together to create a new production.

Paul: Foundation builds bridges between people through theater both within and between different communities. So, for example with those four "B. H." neighborhoods the primary population of each of those neighborhoods is racially specific, and economically specific. Baldwin Hills is African-American upper-middle income, Beverly Hills is European-American upper income, Boyle Heights is a lower-income Latino neighborhood. And the bridge show that Marc was describing brought people together from all the neighborhoods.

Marc: The woman who cofounded Foundation with Paul had a daughter in 1995, and then had a little boy who was born exactly a year before Jamie. Seeing her and her husband, and her children, and how they made it work, how they made being parents work within the context of still being a part of Foundation, was very inspiring to us. The hours alone are much more bizarre than a regular office job. You often have nighttime rehearsals, and weekend rehearsals. And just how they were able to juggle that, it just made it that much more feasible, and maybe not quite so impossible.

Paul: We had both talked about being parents as a couple for quite a while—I can't pinpoint the first time we talked about it. Early on in our relationship the notion that some-day we might have a family was very appealing to both of us. But I think it became much more real when we had a wedding ceremony in 1997, which we'd also talked about for many years. It was a huge production in many ways, and a very, very important event. And I think that freed us up; the fact that we had found a way to publicly celebrate our love, I think, gave us the courage to think more about having a child.

Marc: Speaking of our wedding ceremony, friends of ours had given us a weekend at a beach hotel as a wedding pres-ent, and that weekend was very much about talking about adoption, and about are we really going to do this, and we should just go ahead and start the ball rolling, and talking about the different models that were out there. I think we both felt that . . . it's hard not to sound too cosmic about this, that being gay people—and again this is only for us, this is not for anybody else—but this was the right decision for us as gay people who could not have children biologi-cally with each other, that we felt a kind of responsibility to adopt a nonbiological child, to adopt a child that was already in this world.

Paul: Marc said the word "responsibility" and that's part of it, but I also think we thought of it as an incredible opportunity. Here we were a couple who were infertile because of our sexuality with one another, and therefore we had an opportunity to take care of a baby who was already on this earth who needed us. And that seemed just like a great, great opportunity. We really want to stress we don't feel like any gay person or anybody who does surrogacy or wants a child that's biologically theirs that that's in any way problematic, this was just a very personal decision for us.

Marc: We rejected international adoption because we very much wanted to present ourselves as a family and as a couple, and we knew that by doing an international adoption we would, in most cases, need to act as a single person, and we could not be honest about our relationship. We just didn't feel right about that.

The remarkable thing is we assumed that one of us would have to go through the adoption process as a single person, and we would have to pick which one of us would be the adoptive parent first. And then once that process was finalized and the one of us had been granted custody by the court, then we would have to do a second-parent adoption.

Paul: We were sure we'd have to go through all the expense and all the time, as well as all the sadness of not having that person be an official parent, for a long time.

Marc: We think that thanks to our enlightened governor, God bless him, that the regulations were changed, and so we have actually filed a joint petition for joint custody. And if the petition is granted, we will both go on the birth certificate as his parents, as would a regular married couple. For me, the kind of insanity of the whole debate about gay marriage and granting equal status to gay couples as they've granted to married and straight couples is bananas. Sometimes I get very frustrated that here Paul and I have been together in this committed relationship for sixteen and a half years, and are denied many of the rights of friends of ours who are married couples who have been together two years, or three years, and it's not that their love is any less than ours, but I sometimes feel frustrated, like, "What do we have to do to prove to the state, to the federal government, that we're in it for the long haul?"

Our birthmother had chosen us from our birthmother letter, which presented us very clearly as a couple, and as a family. And so she knew then when she chose us. She knew that she was having a boy, and wanted there to be a strong male role model. And I think she thought, Well, why not have two male role models? Her mother's best friend and boss at her mother's job was gay, and was a very good friend to her mother. So she had had positive experiences with gay folks in her life. It didn't really faze her at all that we were a gay couple. She treated us as a couple from the moment we met her really, which was remarkable, remarkable.

Paul: We thought that as a gay couple we'd probably be in the pool two years before a child might be born who would become ours. It was late January that we wrote our "Dear Birthmother" letter, and we met our birthmother on February 14th. So, we were in the pool two weeks. The fact is we hadn't even copied our letter; it was a draft. The facilitator said, "There's this woman who wants to hear about you, can you send your letter." And we said, "Well, it's a draft," and Marc was doing these really sweet little drawings with little dogs, and houses, and theaters to put all over our letter, and we hadn't copied it with the little drawings. She said, "Just fax me what you've got." So, we did and that's what our birthmom read. We still have the copies—they're beautiful! Our birthmother was the first person who read our "Dear Birthmother" letter, and Jamie was born four months later. So, it all happened so fast for us in a way that took our breath away.

Our birthmother was a twenty-seven-year-old woman who has two children, a six-year-old and a two-year-old, who share a father, but who is a different father than our baby's. She had been in an abusive relationship with the birthfather of our baby. When we met her she was in a shelter for abused women, she and her two kids, and she wanted to place her baby for adoption, she said, both because she did not feel she could handle raising a third child as a single parent and also because she did not feel comfortable raising the child of her abuser.

Marc: But she said a very beautiful thing in the hospital to us, which is that she really believes that her children are innocent, and so that she knew that this baby was innocent of the sins of his biological father. But she also knew that he would be better off raised by other people, because she knew that she had a lot of anger toward this man.

Paul: We saw our birthmother and her two children on the average once a week. And then in the couple of weeks before she gave birth, every other day. We were there at the birth, we were in the delivery room, we each held one hand of our birthmom.

Marc: Paul cut the cord. The two days we spent in the hospital she was very clear about wanting Jamie to be in her room, but she did not want to feed him or change him.

Paul: She wanted Jamie to be in her room with us.

Marc: With us. And so the four of us spent pretty much two days together in the hospital room, which were remarkable, remarkable days, the discussions we had. And even the times we just sat in silence just watching TV together were just really, really extraordinary times.

Paul: She had done a terrific job of explaining to her six-year-old son that we were going to be the baby's dads, and he understood that. I think that emotionally it was a complex thing for him to grasp, but he understood the facts of the situation. The last time that we saw them she said that he was very proud and talked about the fact that he has a little brother who doesn't live with them, but lives with his two dads.

Marc: The times that we saw them after Jamie was born, he always asked to hold Jamie. And every time would turn to his mother and say, "Do you want to hold him?" And she would say, "No, no, that's OK." And then one of the last times he was holding him he said, "Do you want to hold him?" She said, "No, no," and he said, "How come you never hold him?" And it was this moment for Paul and me like, "Ahhh, what is she going to say?" And she handled it so beautifully, she said, "Oh, he's just squirming around. I don't want to hold a squirming baby." You know, she didn't make it into a big issue for her little boy, but she stuck to her guns. It was too complicated, I think, for her to actually hold him.

Paul and I share the same middle name, James, which is how we arrived at our son's first name. We asked our birthmother if she wanted to give him his middle name, and she chose the name of her brother, who was killed in a drive-by shooting ten years ago. He has a little bit of each of us, and a little bit of his birthmother in his name.

Paul: We didn't know if she would be insulted or just not interested in that opportunity, and instead she seemed to be very moved by the opportunity and she took it. Originally, she had great clarity that she wanted pictures sent twice a year to our adoption lawyer, so that her children when they were growing up could go and look at them. She did not only not want contact with us, she didn't even want to see the pictures; she just wanted them to be on file with the lawyer. Over the course of our relationship, before Jamie's birth, we all grew closer and closer, and she first broached the possibility that she might want to see us and the baby after birth. She said that it was still just a remote possibility, but if we would consider it, she wanted to legally have that opportunity, always with our consent.

And we ended up seeing our birthmom and her two kids once a week for the first eight weeks of Jamie's life. Then she and the two kids moved across the country to live with relatives, and that of course simplified the potential emotional complications, in terms of how often we were seeing each other, but also brought great sadness because we were so close. And we plan to stay in each other's lives, and still see each other, but not as often because we now live on opposite sides of the country,

Marc: I think the openness of our adoption is very challenging to both of our families.

Paul: I would say to most people. I was very surprised by very liberal friends who are really thrown by it.

Marc: At first Paul was very attracted by open adoption, and it scared me. I mean, I was terrified.

Paul: We should just be clear linguistically because I know when you refer to "open adoption," there's lots of degrees of open adoption. And I think in particular the notion of a continued visitation of the birthmother with the child and with us, continued relationship with in-person visits, that's what we're talking about right now by using "open adoption" as shorthand.

Marc: That notion was terrifying to me. Because I just thought the emotional complexity of where you draw boundaries was just very difficult to negotiate. I think it's to Jamie's birthmother's tremendous credit that it hasn't been. She's someone we genuinely enjoy spending time with, and we genuinely enjoy spending time with her kids. We're going to take our cues completely from our son in that as he grows older. If having contact with her and seeing her is difficult for him, then we will absolutely make decisions that are in his best interest.

But at this point we can only feel that knowing his birthmother can at this point be healthy for him. Adoption is not a secretive thing, it is not a shameful thing. Understanding the circumstances of her decision to place him with us can only be healthy for him.

Paul: We're doing a show this fall, actually, that Jamie is going to appear in as the Baby Jesus! It's our citywide bridge show, so these are people we're bringing together from all fourteen communities in L.A. that we've worked with over the nine years that we've been here. So, some of these folks were in one or two or even three shows with us already, and I was shocked to realize when Marc pushed in the stroller with Jamie in it, during the first read-through, that a good half of the people in that circle did not know that we were a couple, and did not know that I was gay.

When Marc pushed Jamie in, it was a real moment of truth for me. Because I thought, That's my husband and my son, and I cannot *not* introduce them as my husband and my son. So, it was a big outing moment for me in terms of a good half the people in that circle. As the years have gone on we've become more comfortable and more open and brave; it's been an ongoing process. Jamie is pushing it all—and bless him for it—much farther, much faster in certain circumstances.

Marc: During the rural years of travel with Foundation we found other gay folks in every community we worked in, even the smallest town, and we were open about our sexuality and our relationship in every place.

Paul: But usually to a pretty small handful.

Marc: I think part of it was just a feeling of safety on our part, knowing that there are plenty of people out there who have problems with homosexuality, and not even wanting to go down that road. I think some of our reluctance had to do with some of the assumptions we made, which in retrospect were probably pretty unfair, about rural communities, that people would probably be less accepting. I do have a lot of regret about not being more open about our relationship in those years.

Paul: When the two of us are in public with Jamie and are obviously his parents, it outs you as gay people in a way that I think is one of the completely unexpected, and one of the greatest, gifts that Jamie is giving us. He is helping us be more out, and helping us be braver. And who put it really well? Your brother-in-law. He said we also have a tremendous responsibility to Jamie, because if we ever try to hide the fact that we are a couple from anybody, what an incredible disservice we're doing to our son, to deny the love not only that we have for one another, but especially for him, if we ever tried to hide the fact that we were a couple from anybody.

Marc: To hear my brother-in-law say this very simply—"Well, of course you have to be out for his sake, that's your responsibility"—was really wonderful. Small things we've noticed, even at the supermarket where people will go out of their way to come over and say hello, and say, "Oh, is that your son? How old is he?" And are absolutely showing their support and showing, in not so many words, that they think that this is a good thing. And that has happened again, and again, and again with people in the supermarket, or a baby store. And that's been great, just delightful.

The question of "Where's Mommy?" finally emerged when we were on a plane.

Paul: One of the flight attendants leaned over Jamie while making her way through with the food cart, and said, "Where's Mommy?" to Jamie. And so we explained that we were his two dads, and that his birthmother was in New York. She then proceeded to ask us what we thought of afterward as really personal questions.

Marc: Pretty loudly.

Paul: Pretty loudly, with everybody within a good ten-foot radius being able to hear whether we were Jamie's biological parents.

Marc: What she said was, "Are either of you the dad?" And we answered by saying, "Well, no, his dad is not really in the picture." And of course as we were discussing it afterward we realized we have to be really clear about the semantics of it. We should have said to her, "Well, we're both his dads, but neither of us is his biological father, if that's what you mean." But it just sort of caught us off guard and we realized that for Jamie's sake we have to be very clear about what this means.

Paul: She said, "It's all very modern!"

Marc: "Isn't that neat?" I mean, she wasn't in any way upset about it or judgmental, she just was fascinated by the whole thing.

Paul: We're not so naive. While there are people who come over to support us, I'm sure there's an equal number of people who are silent because they disapprove. Of course, we're going to encounter people throughout Jamie's life who are going to disapprove of our relationship, and disapprove of his adoption, and we know that. But we have had lots, and lots, and lots of affirming, positive experiences. And the fact that Jamie is of a different racial background than we are is all part of the mix.

Marc: There are a couple of states—New Hampshire and Florida are two of them—that don't allow gay and lesbian folks to adopt. I think those laws should be changed. I think that the laws should reflect what is going to be in the best interest of the child. I firmly believe, along with many millions of other people, that a child is best served in a family in which there is a lot of love and support, and generosity and kindness and respect, and that comes in all shapes and sizes. It comes in single-parent households, where there is a single mother or a single dad, and it comes with two moms or two dads, and it comes with two moms and a dad, and other arrangements, and of course it comes with Mom and Dad. I think the proof is in the pudding. If people are opposed to gay adoption they should give us a call, or call other gay parents, or come and see us with our son.

I think that people would be surprised how much our family looks like their family. And that yes, there are two dads in this family, but we get up in the middle of the night to change his diaper, or give him a bottle, or we both take him for a walk around the neighborhood with our dogs, or we go to a friend's house and we bring the baby, and that means we have to be home at nine. It's just like everybody else's life, except that there are two men at the head of this household. I think that we do have a special responsibility as two men raising this child that women be a part of his life, and because there is no mother in this picture, we have a responsibility to make sure that there are positive women role models, and that he has family friends that are women, and that the women in our families are a huge part of his life.

I would also say that one of the most amazing things to me in becoming a parent are all those clichéd things that new parents say, that used to kind of annoy me before, like, "Oh, well it will change your life," or "Oh, your priorities just get completely different." "They grow so fast." Every single thing is true! It does change your life in ways that I'd not even imagined that are miraculous. And if anybody out there is even contemplating it, they should find out more about adoption. Whether or not they can have biological children of their own, they should explore it because it has been life-changing and life-affirming for us in ways that are just unfathomable.

I don't think being a parent is everybody's journey in this life by any means. But adoption should absolutely be an option for everybody. It should be an option for gay couples or gay singles or lesbians. More and more people in the gay and lesbian community are becoming parents and that makes me so happy, and I think that the government should do what it can to encourage that because it encourages family.

Within the gay and lesbian community there are people who believe it's a source of pride to define one's self in op-position to the heterosexual majority. And I absolutely, com-pletely support anyone's decision and choice to live a lifestyle that is defiantly different, and not at all mirroring any type of heterosexual model. Our decision to have a wedding cere-mony and our decision to adopt can certainly be seen by some as aping a heterosexual model. For us it hasn't been about that so much as trying to reinvent what's already out there for us, and for what our family is and for what we want our family to be.

Paul: As there are more and more gay parents—and I have learned this in my own family—prejudice toward gay and les-bian people melts away when a baby is involved. It's just been deeply moving, and true. When a baby's involved the preju-dice just melts away. People can have any sort of abstract prejudices and fears and stereotypes, but when there's a baby involved it's just amazing how love really does conquer the fear.

Update

PAUL AND MARC continue to be unofficial goodwill ambassa-dors for same-sex adoption, and Jamie was a tremendous suc-cess in his first big role as the Baby Jesus.

Comments

PAUL AND MARC were able to be adoptive parents due to a combination of factors: They worked with an open-minded birthmother who accepted who they were, they lived in the State of California, and most important, they lived at a particular time in history.

Well into the 1970s the traditional nuclear family was the only model that states and agencies thought was worthy of the privilege of adoption. That began to change as the divorce rate rose, people married at a later age or just lived together, and never-married women in particular clamored for the right to a family. But if you happened to be single because you were gay, you knew better than to mention it to your social worker if you ever wanted to see an adopted child in your home.

The last fifteen years have brought about important changes in attitudes and practices in many states. Openly gay men and women have been accepted as foster parents, have adopted independently as single people, and in a few states are now allowed to adopt as a couple, with full legal rights. Florida and New Hampshire both expressly forbid adoption by homosexuals under any circumstances, and many other states exercise de facto policies against would-be gay adoptive parents. In 1999 New Hampshire repealed its ban on gay and lesbian adoption, leaving only Florida to bear the standard of intolerance, but several other states are currently considering implementing similar prohibitions.

One of the most significant steps toward allowing nontraditional families to participate in the adoption process took place when second-parent adoptions were first allowed. It worked this way: One of the partners adopted the child, and once the first adoption was final the second partner petitioned the court to adopt the same child. The court allowed the second adoption but did not terminate the rights of the first partner to adopt. They were now coparents with equal rights and responsibilities toward the child, and both of their names were listed on the new birth certificate as parents.

While it was a welcome improvement, there were big problems with second-parent adoptions. If you happened to live in the wrong state the option was unavailable to you; it took approximately two years before the second partner was a legal parent; the home study fees had to be paid twice; and there was always the possibility that the first parent would have a change of heart and not allow the second parent to adopt.

Imagine the pain and problems set in motion when a second-parent adoption was interrupted before finalization because a couple broke up. The first person to adopt could prevent the second parent from ever seeing the child again, even though they had both parented the child since birth. Unlike the protections offered to children in divorce, the child here could not be placed on the second parent's health insurance as a legal dependent, and there would be no child support, no social security benefits if the second parent died, and no inheritance from that parent if he or she died without a will. Delaying the time parental rights were given to the second parent meant huge losses for these children, to whom these would-be parents were "legal strangers" until their part of the adoption was final. California no longer allows these "limited consent" adoptions, and has substituted stepparent adoption for same-sex couples who are registered domestic partners, when one person is already a legal parent.

In response to the problems caused by second-parent adoptions, a handful of states now allow the adoption of a child by a same-sex couple to proceed with both partners on the petition from the time of the child's birth, exactly as it is done for married couples. This is the way Paul and Marc are adopting in California. It offers protections for both partners and for the child.

It is estimated that there are six to fourteen million children being raised in gay unions or households. *Newsweek* magazine's November 1996 cover story was about what some call the "gaybe" boom. Lesbians were being inseminated by sperm donors, or sometimes willing friends, then raising their children with partners while taking steps to officially adopt them. Others were foster parents petitioning to adopt their foster kids. Gay men were taking advantage of surrogacy where there were adoption issues, and many were raising children from prior marriages and wanted their same-sex partner to adopt them as a stepparent would. The children in these unions need and deserve legal protection. The states that ignore this fail to deal with society as it really is. The homosexual community and their progeny are there—not acting on their behalf doesn't make them go away or reduce the risks to their well-being.

Although much headway is being made, there is no room for complacency. In the fall of 2000 the Senate ratified a treaty aimed at curtailing abuses in international adoption. It had been held up for six years by a Republican representative from New Jersey who wanted specific language excluding gays and lesbians from being able to adopt internationally.

Florida again embarrassed itself by allowing gay and lesbian foster parents to nurture HIV-positive children for up to ten years and then threatened to remove one of them from the only home he's ever known so they could be adopted by heterosexual parents. No one could figure out if Florida was saying that gays make good temporary parents but not permanent ones, or simply that they could be used when it was convenient, with the state's moral view temporarily put aside for expediency.

Couples like Paul and Marc help advance acceptance through their public demonstration of themselves as a family. As they said, they are "outed" every time they take Jamie for a walk together in his stroller. Many adoption issues could be resolved if same-sex marriages were legalized, as they just have been in Holland. This seems less likely than the path that most states are on—allowing coparent adoptions and moving eventually to adoptions by same-sex couples.

Not long ago the entire foster care system of the State of Arkansas was placed under court supervision because of the appalling job the state was doing for its children. Arkansas does not allow homosexuals to be foster parents. It's hard to believe that a same-sex household is really worse for children than a child care system so abysmal the federal government had to take it over. The ACLU has brought a suit challenging the ban, but as of this writing it stands.

Because gays and lesbians have endured so much prejudice and intolerance during their lives, I have found them particularly open to and accepting of birthmothers of diverse cultural and racial backgrounds. Paul and Marc were not only open to adopting a multiracial child, they preferred to do so, a choice that reflected the dedication expressed in their work with Foundation Theater of bringing people of different backgrounds together. One lesbian couple I know are the only adopting family I have ever known who agreed to work with an HIV-positive birthmother. They were blessed with a child who did not inherit the infection. This openness is of particular importance in foster care, where the majority of children waiting to be adopted are non-Caucasian and there is a lack of African-American and Hispanic adoptive parents. There are approximately half a million foster children in the United States.

Every study on the issue has determined that a safe, loving household, and not the sexual orientation of the parents, is what enhances life for a child. Studies clearly show that foster care, especially as placement numbers increase, damages children. If the "best interest of the child" argument is to have any meaning, prejudices and outdated policies have to be put aside so that a hard look can be taken at what really helps children and what really hurts them, and action must then be taken.

The gay, lesbian, and transgender populations are here to stay, and are tireless in their fight for civil rights. These rights should include being adoptive parents, with the same protections and privileges given to all adoptive parents and their children.

5

Not So Black and White

"The process itself took away a part of me. Every time
I would go in, another part of me would be gone—bits
and pieces of my heart, bits and pieces of my mind, my
soul. I kept thinking, I'm not going to have anything
left if I keep doing this."

I called my mother because I was depressed. In her usual
way she kept saying, "You're not depressed, you're not depressed." I kept saying, "You know, I am. And in order for
me to deal with it I have to admit it and work with it from
there." She kept saying, "You're not depressed, and the devil
is a liar, and you have to pray." She got into one of her little
trance states and started praying for me.

Finally I decided to tell her what was going on. I told her
I couldn't get pregnant, and I had been to the doctor and they
were telling me my tubes were blocked. They were saying it

had been going on for so long that they didn't know if it was hereditary, but they were thinking that way. She said the doctors didn't know what they were talking about, everyone in our family's fertile. We have a huge, huge family. I have thirty cousins, I think, and me and another cousin are the only two who haven't had kids. She kept saying, "There's no problem."

Maybe it was hard for her to say that she couldn't really help me but she couldn't say, "I feel helpless," so therefore she just kept trying to take things away and say you should not acknowledge them. I guess I called her up just for once for her to be nurturing. She'd never been, so I don't know why I expected that of her, and she just wasn't.

I went to Philadelphia last year to tell my father. I'm not that close to him. I guess I was angry because he never stayed with my mother, and therefore she stayed with this man, her boyfriend, for so long. As I grew up, in my teen years, I had to go to work with my father every weekend. He has an art gallery. He has one of the biggest collections of African art in the world. The museums in New York have tried for years to get stuff from him. He's a Rasta, a vegetarian; the way he carries himself, it's all from the Bible, the Old Testament. He won't tell us, but I think he's about sixty now. He's a very secretive person. He's also a bigot, to put it mildly. He believes that blacks are "it" in society. He believes in that whole Back to Africa movement and Haile Selassie and all that stuff. He doesn't believe in mixing the races. At times he will tell you that he hates anyone who's not black. He'll say it to anybody who wants to hear. To me, he's a racist, he doesn't hide that.

But he sort of reminds me of a Malcolm X, Martin Luther King kind of person. He's very versatile, verbal, articulate; he's a reader. He's very prominent where he's at. In the community people look up to him, he takes care of people. He's a very intelligent man. In that way, I looked up to him. He would just sit down and tell me things when I was growing up, and the more I look back the more I realize he was really paving the way for me.

For instance, when I decided to go to college he wouldn't pay for it. He had the money to do it but he said, "You know, Patrice, I came to this country, I had nothing, I had absolutely nothing. In order for me to have something I had to work very, very hard doing things that I didn't want to do, and that's the only way I could get to this point in my life. In order for you to appreciate everything in your life, you're going to have to work for it, no one's going to give it to you on a silver platter. If you want to go to school, you're going to have to pay your way and work for it."

When I did my bachelor's I took out loans, and I worked and went to school. I just saved all my money. When I decided to get my master's he laughed. He said, "You don't think I'm going to help you, do you? If this is something that you want, you'll work for it." I resented him for having so much and not giving any to me. But when I look back now, I'm happy he didn't give me anything. I always had a plan, and that's what my dad helped me do. You don't sit back and wait for people to do things for you. He gave me a sense of independence, a sense of self that you just have to work real hard. I appreciate things a lot more because everything I have, I worked for.

So anyway, I went to Philadelphia to tell my father. I thought his reaction was going to be horrible, because he believes in having kids. He truly believes that the only reason to get married and to have sex is to have kids. It was really hard for me to tell him this.

I just walk in on people, I never tell them I'm coming anywhere. So, I walk in on him, I went over and started talking to him and finally I said, "I need you to come outside the store, I need to talk to you about something." So I told him. He just said, "Patrice, why do you want to have kids? It's so hard." He was so much more sympathetic and empathetic than my mother was. He was so nurturing, the very thing that she wasn't. He says, "It's going to be OK, and if I can help in any way, I will." For once in his life he was there for me, and I don't know why but I started crying.

He's very much into medicine and the old way of doing things with the chiefs, because he spent a lot of time in Africa. He knows every medicine man in Africa. He brought in a medicine man, one of these big chiefs; he didn't speak English so he had an interpreter with him. My father said that he was there the week before and he said, "I smell your daughter in this store." My father said, "My daughter lives in California, she is not coming out here." And he says, "Oh, there's something going on with her." This was the week before, and then I walk in. That's why my father was like, "Ah!"

So he was telling me, "This guy's coming, this guy's coming, just wait. He's going to be shocked when he sees you."

So I waited a couple of hours and he showed up. He just took one look at me and said, "Oh, this is your daughter." I sat down with him and he was asking me what was going on so I told him and he said, "You know, there's medicine that can help you, from Africa." But my father didn't follow through with it because he would have had to go there and get the medicine. I said to my father, "I can't go to Africa!" He goes there all the time, he has property there. This wife that he has now, she's from Uganda. So every time I call him I go, "Did you take care of that for me yet?" He goes, "Don't worry, I'll take care of it." So I've been waiting for him to take care of it.

It took me a long time to tell my friends about infertility because my mom and dad said you keep everything inside, you just don't talk to people. It took me a long time to be able to talk to anyone else outside of my husband and my family. But I told my friend Margaret, who I've known for a long time. She's been waiting forever for us to have a kid because she's already pronounced herself godmother. So I told her, and it was the reaction you read about in the books— you know, "Do they know what they're talking about? . . . I can't believe this is happening"—and she was really good for a little while. Then she was saying, "I know someone who got pregnant anyway, people who just relax get pregnant, and maybe if you have a vacation you'd get pregnant." I said, "We've been thinking about adoption." She goes, "The minute you adopt, you're going to get pregnant." I kept thinking, Why did I tell her? I told my other friend, who's from Jamaica. We've always understood each other; she's never judged or made any comments like that. She was just really, really sad. She's probably the one friend I can talk to about it without any judgments, or any kind of statements that are insensitive.

For a long time I thought that I couldn't get pregnant, even before the infertility workup. In the back of my mind I knew that there was something wrong, though my husband kept saying otherwise. The infertility medications, and what they did to me, and in terms of my hormones—I felt that they were just out of whack. I would just get so sick. Constantly having to go and subject yourself to these people looking inside of you every single day—they do ultrasounds every day—and the shots. You do it when you have your period, and then you just do it continuously during the course of the whole infertility workup. I didn't like that at all because it wouldn't be the same physician every time, it was a series of physicians. When you're at a teaching hospital that's what happens, but I didn't do real well with that.

I work at a top university hospital. It was hard because I worked around the corner from where I was getting infertility treatments. Every time I had to go to that floor there were certain exits and entrances I wouldn't go through. I avoided them totally because I could run into the people from the infertility clinic. Here's your whole personal life being exposed. Anyone could pick up your chart and look at it. I believe in confidentiality and privacy and I was coming in there and all of that was taken away from me.

People don't realize it's like a roller coaster. You go up and down, up and down. One day everything is fine, you think everything's going to work out, and the next day it just falls apart. I couldn't deal anymore. Men go through it differently. You're someplace but they're someplace else, and it means something different to them because they're not going through the infertility therapy you're going through. They don't understand the pain, the heartache. I think they really try to, but sometimes you can't even explain it.

For most people pregnancy happens and they have no control over it, so they figure that everyone should be able to have kids when they're ready. Other people think it has something to do with *you*: "You need to have more rest." I mean the things that they come up with—they're blaming me! My mom believes that God will take care of everything in your life. She felt that because I was not born-again like she was, that that was one of the reasons I was going through what I was going through, and that if I got saved that everything would be all right. She also made some comment about someone in the Bible who had kids at ninety years old, and there was still hope because I was only in my thirties, so there was nothing I had to worry about.

The process itself took away a part of me. Every time I would go in, another part of me would be gone—bits and pieces of my heart, bits and pieces of my mind, my soul. I kept thinking, I'm not going to have anything left if I keep doing this. It just made me more sensitive; I didn't want to be bothered with anything or anyone. I didn't want to talk to anyone, I wouldn't tell people what I was going through—I felt like no one would understand. I was depressed from the moment it started till I made the decision I can no longer do this. I don't think that there was anything positive in infertility and the subsequent treatments. It was the hardest thing I ever had to do. It was a really painful time in my life. I never want to see another doctor; I haven't been to the doctor since. I just can't bring myself to do that. Two weeks ago I had food poisoning, my stomach was killing me. I thought of every reason why I should not go to the hospital and I laid in bed sick, I refused to go.

Adoption had always been in the back of our minds from the moment we realized we're probably not going to be able to have kids of our own. The thing that really bothers me is if you decide to have a child and you're able to do it in a natural way, no one does any fingerprints, no one checks your tax returns, no one checks for references. But if you want to adopt, they do all of this. So what makes them think that I'm not going to be a good parent just because I'm not having this child naturally?

We didn't tell many people we were going to adopt. People didn't accept the infertility thing—how would they accept this? At first we were going to adopt a baby from India, but then we found out what that entailed. Then we decided to adopt from Jamaica, since I was from there and one parent had to be Jamaican. We went to Jamaica and that was really hard, because we wanted a little girl and we found out that Jamaicans don't give up their girls. Every place where we went where they had kids, they were all boys. We went into these agencies and there were just boys everywhere, tons of boys. It was so sad because when we were leaving they were like, "Please, take me with you!" They were crying and running after us. I just kept saying, "I can't do this." Because if you take one, you feel like you should just take all of them with you.

In most cultures, boys provide. But in Jamaica, the girls are the ones who take care of their parents. It's a society where the women are very, very powerful. They take care of the family—they work, they cook, they do everything. So it's real important to have daughters.

Anyway, we eventually decided to go through an adoption agency here in the States that was of no cost to us, with the exception of the fingerprints. They put us through hell for a year and a half. First they told us that we had to go through an orientation, but we thought of it as disorientation. We were falling asleep, because it took hours. Their main focus was not adoption, it was foster care, which was quite annoying to us because they touched on adoption maybe twice, if that many times.

They told us someone would be in contact with us. It was a long time before we got something in the mail saying we had to go through parenting classes. The parenting class was going to be four or five weekends for five hours each time. I called and said, "Look, my husband is a physician, he sometimes works seven days a week, he works on weekends and there's no way we can make it to those classes. Is there something we can work out, maybe during the week after work or something?"

No one got back to me for a couple of months. I contacted them again and I said, "Look, we really want to do this but we're having a really hard time. I'm sure you have to be able to work something out to adjust to schedules. I'm sure he's not the first one who's ever come up with this." They didn't get back to us. I have a friend who is on the board of directors, I told her about this whole thing. Apparently she spoke with the head of the agency, and all of a sudden we got a phone call. Everyone forgot about the parenting class we had to go to. It was never an issue; we never had to do it. They assigned us a social worker right after she called.

We met with the social worker, she did our home visits, we got all our paperwork in, which was enormous, got our fingerprints in. The fingerprints took five months. First they misplaced them. There was another piece of paper that was supposed to go with it—they forgot to do that. It was going to take another five months. Everything that we were supposed to get in, we did, including our references. The social worker looked in our files—everything was in. Then I got a phone call from the assistant director. She said, "I'm going to look through your file." Then she called me up and told me I had nothing in my file, they had lost or misplaced everything.

This agency was set up to help minority families—black, that is—to adopt. They said there aren't enough black families out there. I couldn't believe they put us through hell. This went on for a year. Whenever I called I was put through to the assistant director. I asked, "What's going on?" She told me, "I notice that you're seeing a therapist and I need a letter from your therapist to make sure that you're OK." She said that this was the reason for the holdup. I just blew my top. I said, "I want to withdraw everything I ever put into your agency, and *I* will take this further. I want you to send all my paperwork back."

They were not doing their jobs. They never talked about a child. The more I think back, the more I keep thinking, Where were they going to get this child from? There was never an effort; it was all focused on paperwork. They said, "You don't have to pay any money." But they don't do anything. I'd rather pay the money and have something done than not pay the money and nothing's done.

We decided to do private adoption. I came to the point where I said we were going to have to find the money from somewhere. I worked it all out later and determined the expenses for the birthmother to come here, her medical expenses, the attorney and the facilitator fees were about $10,000.

I'd heard most people are successful with private adoptions. I felt like this was going to happen. But you always have that thing in the back of your mind that nothing else has worked, so maybe this won't work. We decided we didn't want to go through the newspaper ads and all of that if we could hire a facilitator to do it for us. A facilitator finds birthmoms; she does the advertising, but she is paid for the service. We would speak with the birthmothers and decide who we wanted to work with.

One thing that the facilitator told us was that we would probably not find a pure black baby. She told us because of cultural reasons a lot of blacks don't give up their babies. Often with mixed-race children there is some racism connected with giving up the baby because of where they live or family pressure. Some of the moms are very young, and they feel that they can't take care of the baby. Our birthmother was fifteen years old, was in the ninth grade, and lived in Mississippi. I think it took her a while to tell her family. The birthmother was Spanish and French, but the birthfather was black. When she did tell her family about the pregnancy they decided they were going to keep the baby. Or, if her parents weren't willing to do that, her sister was going to do that for her and just keep the baby with her family.

Everything was fine and dandy until one day she wrote a letter to her sister saying, "I can't talk to you about this and I can't talk to Mom and Dad about this." It said, "Read this after I'm gone." The letter basically said that the guy was black. Mississippi is still, I guess, a very racist place because her sister made several remarks to me, one of which is that they would have to leave if they kept the baby there. They live in a very, very small town and one girl had a baby and it was mixed and the family had to leave town. The other remark she made to me was that if her father found this guy he would kill him, and in Mississippi he would get away with it. The interesting thing is that after she told me all of this, she asked what race we were. I said, hesitantly, "Black." And she goes, "Oh, oh."

She was basically saying that they had no choice but to give this baby up. They had called around in Mississippi and no one was willing to take a mixed child. Actually, before they did that they went for her to have an abortion. They found out that she was seven months pregnant, she couldn't have an abortion. Even though they were Roman Catholics, once they found out this baby was mixed they were willing to get rid of it any way possible. They kept saying, "You don't have to worry about us changing our minds." I felt they were telling the truth.

After our daughter was born, it took me about five weeks to tell my dad. I guess the reason why I couldn't tell him was the whole racial thing. I knew how he would feel about it because of one of my cousins. She was in a mixed marriage, and her daughter was about my daughter's complexion. I remember being in his store and this little girl came in with her grandmother and he wouldn't acknowledge her because she was mixed. That stayed in my mind, and I just couldn't call him.

Finally, I got up enough guts to call him, to talk to him about it. My expectation was we were going to get into this whole race issue; I'm not going to beg him to accept her. I finally said, "We adopted." He said, "Well, why'd you do that?" He says, "Is there something wrong with your husband?" I said, "No. Don't you recall that we had a conversation and I told you that my tubes were blocked?" Then he said, "Haven't you been watching the news or reading the paper about that Jessica baby and what happened with that? How could you do something like that knowing that this could happen?"

Then he said, "What color is that baby?" I said, "The baby's a human being." So we didn't get very far with that. He says, "I just want to let you know that I have nothing to do with that baby, that's not my genes." Because I said to him, "You know, you're a grandfather." He goes, "I am not a grandfather, that is NOT my genes." And that was the end of our conversation.

Initially I had a hard time with it. It took me a couple days to finally say, "It's OK." I will never expose her to him because I don't think she deserves that. She's an innocent child in the midst of all this. We just won't acknowledge him as a grandfather, period.

Update

PATRICE'S FATHER HAS come to accept the new baby as Patrice's child, but will not refer to her as his granddaughter. Patrice and her husband have decided not to adopt a second child.

Comment

PEOPLE DO NOT like to talk about the racial issues in adoption for fear of being called racist, but it is too important an adoption topic to ignore. Passions run high on the subject, but there are certain facts that those who work in adoption do not dispute. For example, African-American and to a lesser degree Hispanic women place their children for adoption less often than Caucasian women in independent adoption. Traditionally, Hispanic and African-American families have kept any unplanned or "unwanted" children within the extended family. There is a shame attached to adoption in these communities that often outweighs all other considerations, such as poverty, the birthmother's desire to place the child, or even her aversion to being a parent. There is a slightly higher risk of a birthmother's changing her mind if she is a member of either of these groups.

The question of race always arises in adoption; it usually comes up in the first consultation an adoptive family has with an attorney. The surprise is that the racial issues are not what one might expect. What adoptive parents of all races say is, "We would like a child who sort of looks like us." People are not antiwhite, anti-African-American or anti-Hispanic when it comes to welcoming a child into their home. It is more of a privacy issue—they resent the constant casual inquiries of strangers. From those who have adopted from a racial group other than their own I hear, "I would just like to go to the store once without some perfect stranger coming up to me and saying, 'Is that your kid?' I don't want to have to discuss my personal life with everyone I meet." As we see from Patrice and her husband's story, there can be nonacceptance of a child because of race from any ethnic group.

In an independent adoption, the birthmother has always been able to choose the race of the adoptive family. But it was only in 1996 that the official policy of race matching was dropped by the public adoption agencies. (Children are available to adopt through the public adoption agencies when the state has removed them from their parents' care for abuse, abandonment, or neglect and terminated the rights of the parents.) For years, fueled by the convictions of groups like the National Association of Black Social Workers, public agencies would not place a child of one race with an adoptive family of another race. The problem was that most of the children waiting to be adopted through the public agencies were African-American or Hispanic and the majority of the waiting adoptive parents were Caucasian. With race the dominant issue, children were condemned to a life of foster care. The policy has been changed so that race may be considered as one factor in the matching of child to prospective parents, but not as the only or determining factor. This change is of great importance. In Los Angeles County alone there are fifteen to twenty thousand children in foster care, many of whom are waiting to be adopted.

Although the official racial policies of the public agencies have changed, ambivalence still exists in cultural attitudes toward transracial adoption. Transracial adoption refers to the adoption of a child of one race by an adoptive family of another, but most people use the term to mean adoption of African-American children by Caucasian families. That is how I will use it here. In one recent eight-week period I experienced three incidents related to transracial adoptions, all of which occurred at the hospitals at the time of birth. In the first instance a twenty-six-year-old African-American birthmother who had just delivered her fourth child allowed herself to be pressured into keeping the child—after having made an adoption plan—by two nurses at the hospital where she delivered. They told her that adoption was a bad thing, and that she should not place her child with the Caucasian adoptive family she had chosen under any circumstances, even though that family had adopted several African-American children. They delivered their message during the difficult three-day period she spent in the hospital recovering from a cesarean birth. They also brought the child to her several times, despite her written request not to see the child after birth. She said to me of this child, "People ask me what I named her. I say, 'I haven't given her a name.' They say, 'That's terrible,' and all this stuff. But I am not *into* this child!" Nonetheless, she kept the baby.

In the second instance a Caucasian adoptive mom was intentionally misinformed by the hospital social worker about the sixteen-year-old African-American birthmother who wanted to place her child into the woman's racially mixed family. The social worker told the adoptive mother to go home because the birthmother was wavering, and probably wouldn't place her child. The adoptive mother was also told she "didn't exist" as far as the hospital was concerned, and was treated accordingly. The birthmother had never said she was wavering, and felt confused and upset at this needless drama.

In the third instance the hospital social workers lied to and refused to cooperate with the attorney, the adoption agency, and the adoptive family. They would not supply necessary paperwork, and misrepresented their authority on legal issues, telling the adoptive mother they had the power to take the child if they chose. They visited the birthmother repeatedly, telling her, in that familiar refrain, that adoption was a bad thing, especially when an African-American child goes into a Caucasian home. The birthmother was poor, and lived in a neighborhood where she feared for her safety because of frequent drive-by shootings; the birthfather was a felon wanted by the FBI. These facts were ignored by those trying to influence her. It all came down to race. The quality of life for the adopted child, the birthmother, and the children she already had was not considered. None of this is meant to dismiss the potential problems or challenges that exist when a family of one race raises a child of another, but if the alternative to adoption is a life of poverty and neglect or foster care, the balance clearly weighs in favor of a stable home. All other questions concerning how a child is taught about or introduced to his or her cultural heritage are secondary.

Although racist attitudes can only be fought over time, through education and experience, the ultimate solution to this specific problem is finding African-American families to adopt African-American children.

The agency that Patrice dealt with has a rule that no birthmother may receive money to assist her with her living expenses, even though she is allowed to accept it by law. Its policy is to forbid any exchange of money between the birthmother and the adoptive family, claiming it is suggestive of baby buying, and reminiscent of the purchase of slaves. I have found few people outside of this agency who think that providing a poor, pregnant woman with food, clothing, and shelter is baby buying, much less slavery, though there are still some states that forbid the payment of living expenses. The agency employees who advocate against this humanistic aid are themselves paid for their efforts, even when their work is sloppy and ineffectual, as they were with Patrice and her husband.

In the early days of my practice I called this agency several times to find adoptive families for the African-American birthmothers who contacted me and specifically requested African-American families. They always declined to help because the birthmothers needed financial assistance. I had to turn these women away, telling them that I could find no home for their children, knowing that there was a long waiting line of African-American adoptive families at this agency.

6

Why Don't They Want My Baby?

MICHELLE

A birthmother

**"All you can think about is, Oh, I'm going to have such
a cute little baby. That's where I was at: He's going to
be so cute."**

*My mom and dad did a lot of drugs. From what I un-*derstand, my mom was really into acid, and just really into
her own little world. My dad raised me all by himself from
the time I was three, because my mother left my brother and
me. My mom had a three-year-old and a nine-month-old at
eighteen. I remember her giving us a hug and putting on her
coat and saying, "Bye, I'm going to be gone for a little while."
She put bottles all over the place for my brother to find and
she just left us. My dad was gone for the weekend and came
home a day and a half later and saw us two kids sitting in the
house. My brother was sitting in a diaper that was a day and
a half old; I didn't know how to change him.

My dad depended on my grandmother a lot, we always lived close to Grandma. So my grandmother's like my mom, my best friend, the only woman that I look up to. She's so feisty, she just stands on her own. She's very independent, very strong. There are some times that she just embarrasses me because she's just so bold and open with what she feels about people. But I also admire that too, that she's got the balls and the self-confidence that she doesn't care.

A lot of people don't like me, so I have to start building that characteristic. I think I give people the wrong impressions about me. They say that people think I'm very stuck-up and a snob, but I'm not. I've probably been raised in much worse conditions and am stupider than they are, but I walk with my head high and don't care.

When I found out I was pregnant this time, my fifth time, my whole family told me, "You're making the biggest mistake of your life if you keep him; you can't do it." It was hurtful, but it probably helped me too. I think if everybody in my family kept telling me, "Have him and everything will be OK," I'm sure I would have had him and kept him. But if everybody's telling me that adoption's the best way and all the adoption alternatives and how things will be better for me, if people are telling you that all the time, it's much easier to do.

At the time I got pregnant, I was married, but separated, and was twenty-three years old. I had two kids and I had just moved into my grandmother's house. I'd been separated from my husband, John, for over two years. John and I never had a big falling-out; I just left him and he let me leave him and he never saw anybody else. He took the kids every other weekend and we were still very friendly to each other.

When we had been married four years we moved back to L.A. from Santa Barbara. I started working, at a beer bar, basically, pool and loud music and stuff, where I met up with all my old buds. It was the first time I'd worked through our whole marriage. I started managing that place, and that's where I met Mac. I met Mac thinking, Oh my God, this is true love and I'm going to leave my husband for him, and I'm going to marry Mac. I just totally fell in love.

We used to get really out of control with each other, and it was nothing but being totally possessive. It was so twisted, it got really obsessive. It started getting like this about six months into our relationship and we didn't break up for two years.

About four months into seeing Mac, before things started getting really bad, I started seeing Stan, this baby's father. Stan and I started seeing each other every day, every night, almost immediately. Stan and I had the agreement that we're going to be best friends and we're going to sleep together too because that's fun, you know? We didn't want any commitment. We both promised from the beginning not to feel anything, but you always do and you don't realize it.

We were just friends and never ever intended to have a baby. Then, right about the time I found out I was pregnant, Stan started seeing someone else. He came over one night and he wanted to talk to me, and broke up with me that night, and that same night I tell him I'm pregnant.

We sat up until four-thirty in the morning and talked about

that we were going to keep it, that we were going to raise it and that he was going to get used to my kids, he was going to marry me, and I was going to divorce John, and we have to start getting ready for the baby. We fell asleep on my grandma's couch, woke up in the morning, looked at each other, and said, "What the hell were we talking about the night before?" Because it was so unrealistic. He'll never get used to my kids. I don't want my kids to ever get used to another man. I'm just happy with my husband as far as being father to my kids. Stan didn't want to take on the responsibility and I don't want him to. He doesn't know about kids. Stan and I never intended to have anything serious, ever. I mean, I would never say to somebody, "Stan is my boyfriend."

About seven months into my pregnancy he called and said, "I just wanted to see how you're doing and tell you I'm so sorry that I broke up with you." I'm like, "Well, I'm six and a half months pregnant with your child, only you haven't cared to call me or think about me for six and a half months knowing I'm pregnant. Now you've broken up with your girlfriend and you're lonely, you're calling me up." He was all, "Yeah, I'm so sorry. Is there any way I can make up all this time?" I'm like, "No." But then, like always, I went up and saw him and Stan and I slept together when I was almost seven months pregnant. He felt the baby kick and everything. It was hard; we both cried a lot. But at the same time the decision had already been made. I was well into my pregnancy; it was already decided. I saw him that one Saturday night and then I didn't talk to him again until I had the baby.

Before that I was going to have an abortion. I had my

money together, my $150, and Stan wrote me a check for $150. I would make an appointment and I'd end up having something else to do and calling and canceling and rescheduling. I think I was doing it almost mentally on purpose because it's not fun. And I kept putting it off and putting it off, until I put it off too long. So then I wasn't able to have an abortion. It's almost like my subconscious just kept making me not do it.

I'd already had two abortions. I had my first two kids and then I got pregnant with Mac's baby. Mac and I were going to get married, during the good part of everything, but we both felt it was too soon, so I had an abortion. That one was superhard because I had already known what it's like to have kids. That one was very, very hard. Then I had an abortion about eight months later because I was seeing Mac, and I was seeing Stan, and I got pregnant and I didn't know whose it was. So rather than have to tell either one of them or try to explain it, I had a second abortion. I had a really good friend, a male friend, who had the money and he understood where I was at, and he paid for it.

They were so hard that I think that's why I kept putting off having a third one. I knew whose baby it was, and we meant a lot to each other. Just knowing it was Stan's, I couldn't do it. I thought I was going to keep it. When I went over to see Stan and he saw I was still pregnant he said, "I gave you a hundred fifty dollars; you told me you were going to do this. What happened?" And I said, "Stan, I'm sorry, I can't help it, I'm going to have this baby and I'm going to raise him." Stan started yelling at me, "Don't you know what you're doing? You and I aren't going to be together and you should put it up for adoption."

I told John, my husband, in McDonald's Playland about being pregnant. I had taken him and the kids to McDonald's and I told him that I needed to talk to Stan; Stan lived right down the street. I came back in half an hour to pick up John and the kids and I had been crying. And John said, "What's the matter? Why are you crying? What happened with him?" I said, "Well, I might as well tell you now, I'm already crying about it—I'm pregnant." He said, "What?" I was about five and a half months pregnant but I wore long shirts and jeans to keep it hidden. Then he said, "Well, what are you going to do about it, Michelle?" I answered, "I don't know. Stan wants me to put it up for adoption, and I think I'm going to. I've already talked to a few people about it, and I think I'm going to do it." He said, "Good. Because I swear to God you will never see me again. It's too unfair to my kids—you can't do it."

He didn't want me to have the baby. He did not feel it was fair to my kids for me to get pregnant and to have another baby and for me to bring a third party into this whole thing. Also he told me, "You told me years and years ago that you would never, ever have children from more than one man and that you always looked down on girls who say, 'This is my boyfriend's kid, and this is my ex-husband's kid,' you know. You've always looked down on that. Are you going to do that now?"

Because I've always been very proud of the fact that I have two children from my husband and that's it and I'm still married. And he was right. John was right and Stan was right, that I should give him up for adoption. So I agreed: "You're right, you're right." It's like they both broke me down, and kind of brought me back down to the ground that I couldn't have him. They helped me see the total picture, but painfully. I just had this little fantasy, I'm going to have him, oh, it'll be great. Stan said, "Michelle, I see you pull your hair out sometimes with the two that you have." And you don't think about those things. All you can think about is, Oh, I'm going to have such a cute little baby. That's where I was at: He's going to be so cute.

I was living with my grandmother and I was just working part-time. I didn't know really what I was going to do. I didn't know what was going to happen next. I didn't have the means to take care of him, and until everything was made clear to me, I didn't really care if I had the means, I was just going to have him anyways. My two kids are eating and they're fine, and Grandma will take care of the baby too. Then Grandma told me, "No, you're not going to keep living with me and just keep having babies."

So I kept bugging my dad, "OK, Dad, you guys want me to do this. If I should put this baby up for adoption we should start working on it now, because I'm five months pregnant." So Dad mentions Rene. She was the receptionist at his work. She came over and talked to me because my dad said, "Well, my daughter's pregnant and thinking about adoption, why don't you go over and talk to her." So that's how I met Rene and Bob.

She seemed very nice and I'd gotten such a high opinion

of them from my grandmother and my dad. I didn't necessarily like them, it was kind of more like we were matched up together and I just never looked any further. But of course with me it has to be rocky, it can't work out smoothly. God does not shine on me, or the sun doesn't shine, or something doesn't shine. I have had bad luck sometimes.

They had been working on adopting another little baby boy, Adam, two years old, since he was six months old, through the state. So after a year and a half of fighting for this little boy, they'd gotten the news that they'd got him, right about the time they were going to adopt my baby. Rene comes over, she says, "Well, we got Adam, but we're going to adopt your baby too." I said, "OK." I didn't really like the idea because I wanted parents who didn't have kids, but I thought, OK, at least it'll be two *adopted* kids, so it won't be too much partiality.

Then she came over the next day after that, crying and saying that the state wouldn't let her adopt two children and that she sat up the whole night before and thought about it, and decided that she's going to pick Adam, and she doesn't want my baby. I didn't understand it. I mean, she was as kind as she could be; she was crying. She didn't say she didn't want my baby, but she said, "We've decided to adopt Adam." I started crying. I didn't yell at her or tell her I was pissed, but I was pissed.

I felt like I was led on or something, even though I wasn't. It made me really mad. I didn't understand why in the very beginning when they decided they were interested in adopting my baby, and they were already pursuing Adam, why they didn't immediately look into whether they could adopt two children if Adam were to come. They should have prepared for that and figured that out from the beginning, but they didn't until after a month and a half of saying that they are going to take my baby.

I didn't personally feel rejected, I felt like they were rejecting my baby. I just couldn't understand why they were giving up a newborn for a two-year-old. But at the same time, they'd been working on the two-year-old for a year and a half and maybe that's who they were more attached to. I think it worked out for the best, but why it had to come about as it did . . . just my luck.

I'm really glad that they didn't adopt my baby because they only lived four miles away from me. It would be way too hard. I thought I could handle it, but I don't think I could have. To be honest, if it would have come to the very later months of my pregnancy and I still had Rene and Bob as my adoptive parents, I probably would have replaced them or asked them to move. Because as my pregnancy went on I was becoming more and more attached to the baby. I'm sure I would have realized there's no way I can give a baby up and have the baby live four miles away.

I had to find some more parents. I think that's what made me upset more than anything. I looked at some adoption resumes, and honestly, I didn't like any of them, but I interviewed three of the couples. Actually, the first couple I really did like. Stan and I went together to interview them, met them at the park, and talked. They were very nice, but they had their own daughter and that still bothered me. Because it's their own daughter, it's their own flesh and blood and I would fear partiality toward their born child. And even if it didn't happen, it's just something that I didn't want to have to fear when I gave up my baby. I wanted my baby to be THE one. If they had any other children, they would have to be adopted too. I just didn't like the fact that they had their own flesh-and-blood daughter.

The second one seemed nice too, met me at a restaurant right next door to my dad's house. But she brought pictures of their baby right before she died and went into so much detail and stuff about everything that had happened to her and she was crying and breaking down. That just bothered me and made me wonder about her stability. I felt like I had room to be picky, and I just was. If it wasn't perfect, then I wasn't going to do it.

So now I went and saw the third couple. They were so weird. They brought me one picture and it was a picture of the bedroom they were going to have the baby in. And it was just a bedroom and it had a queen-size bed and a computer over on the wall. She said, "Well, you see, we're going to turn it into a nursery." I thought, Then why are you just bringing me a picture of the bedroom? She brought me fresh herbs out of her garden in a plastic grocery sack, and she gave me a copy of her book, which was very interesting. But she wouldn't drink the water from the restaurant; she had her own water. She wouldn't order anything from the restaurant either; she pulled her own salad out of a Baggie and asked them for a plate. He husband ordered a cheeseburger and a

Coke; he was much younger than she was. They were just too strange for me.

My best friend from Santa Barbara told me about Jackie and David. I called her and said, "Go ahead and have your friends call me." Within five minutes Jackie was on the phone. They came to my dad's house about a half hour later and they just seemed so normal, they just seemed perfect. They didn't bring me a picture of a bedroom, they brought me photo albums, showed me their family, showed me their home, showed me their cars, showed me their dogs, showed me their backyard, showed me everything. They explained everybody in their family. I mean, I can still picture what their family looks like.

I remember I made up this list of questions. I sat with my paper and asked questions of all these couples. It was about six pages long—how long had they been married, where did they meet, why did they get married, do they have any children, where do they live, how long have they lived there, where do they work, what do they intend to do for work after the baby's born, what is their religion, what is their family's religious background. Not that it mattered to me, it's just, I'm Christian—I was looking for somebody that was going to raise the baby like I would if I were able to. I just wanted somebody that would have done it like I did it, and they seemed that way.

The interview went really well and they were very, very nice. They got ready to leave and I remember looking at them; I said, "Well, I'll give you guys a call tonight, but I think I'm going to choose you." They said, "How do you know already?" I said, "You should feel good that I'm telling you right now. I can feel it in my gut, I think I'm going to be calling you guys."

I felt the most comfortable with them, I liked everything they told me, and they came from a good reference. I don't think they're going to come more ideal than Jackie and David. I really like David, I like his personality—he's very, very warm. He was just so casual and down-to-earth and just seemed that he's going to race around the carpet with the kids. Jackie seemed very prim and proper and I thought, OK, she'll be a good mom. She was much more aloof and cool, but I think that was more her nerves and stuff. Because then I met her when I was in labor and the girl cut loose.

The birthfather went with me to interview the first couple and then he said that I could handle it by myself, so I just did. I called him afterward and told him that I had chosen people, told him about them, but he had nothing to do with my decision or my reasons for picking them. I had a hundred percent say as far as who I picked.

I had all the rules and stuff set up before I had the baby. I said, "When the baby's born I want you to hold him up to me so that I can see that he's healthy, and then I want him taken out of the room, and I want that to be it." That was supposed to be the arrangement, and I'm still mad about it to this day. I had him, and they didn't take him out of the room; he was in the room for at least fifteen minutes after I had him.

I kept telling them to get him out and they said, "Well, we can't, all the equipment is right here for us to clean him up."

I'm like, "I told you guys that this was the arrangement. You should have taken the equipment into another room and been prepared," but they weren't. I kept yelling, "Get him out! Get the baby out!" I was crying and bawling my eyes out at the same time and I was just, "Get him out, get him out." And Jackie and David kept telling me, "We're trying to get them to get the baby out." I couldn't stand it. So the fifteen minutes after I had him, while the doctor was sewing me up and stuff, the baby was right behind my head crying. That was the hardest part. I felt like if they would have just given him to me he would have been fine. But that's not what I wanted, I wanted them to take him out. They never did give him to me, but I had to sit there and listen to him cry.

Then, they wouldn't move me to a regular ward, because there were no beds; I had to stay in maternity too. When the babies were crying in the nursery, I didn't know which one was mine. It was the first time that I felt so detached from it—I didn't know what his cry sounded like. Stuff like that still bothers me, that I don't know what he smells like, that bothers me a lot—you know, that I don't know what he's like.

My friend Denise held him, and that made me cry too. I asked, "What did he feel like?" I wanted to hold him so bad, but I didn't want to hold him. I know if I did it would have been worse. I wouldn't have given him up. I know it. I wouldn't have, because I would have fallen in love with him. I mean, I already did, you know what I mean, I already did. I think I made the right decision, but I just wish it could have been different. I hate talking about this so much; it makes me want to cry.

It's hard for me to be happy. Nobody understands it. It's part of me, and so talking about it shouldn't be any big deal. But nobody wants to talk about it, which is probably the best thing, because otherwise I'd probably spend my whole life crying. It's gotten easier as far as when I first had him and stuff. Then, at least every other day for some reason, I'd just break down and cry for a couple of hours. It's not like that anymore. It only happens once in a while if I'm just by myself and for some reason get into thoughts of him or something. I don't even really talk about him to anybody, except Denise. But Denise is already to the point where she just avoids it because she knows I get upset about it.

If anybody had asked me, if they were pregnant, and had asked me if they should give it up for adoption, I couldn't answer that for them. It all depends on their own circumstances. I tell anybody that it's not as easy as you think at first. I thought it was going to be easier than it is. I feel like I had total control over the adoption. I felt like I did it the way I wanted to do it. I think that the quicker it's done, the easier it is, at least for the birthmom. Well, probably for the adoptive parents too, because they probably feel secure, like the baby's theirs. It didn't really make any difference to me if I signed the consent to the adoption or not. I'm sure it did to Jackie and David. But to me it was, like, as soon as I gave him up in the hospital I felt like I gave him up, I felt like I was done.

Everything that I did, I did for him and me—although I

feel like I didn't do it for me because of the way I feel now, so sad and stuff. But at the same time, I know I did what was best for everyone. But I didn't know how bad it would be; I didn't know how hard it would hit me. But I wouldn't change it either. I totally recommend getting pictures and getting updates on the baby. It helps me feel I'm still connected to him even if I don't see him. I have to still know about him. I don't remember exactly how much my photo request is, but I wish I could change it so I could receive them more often. Right now he's going through so many changes, he changes every single month, and it bothers me not knowing what he looks like month to month.

I'd like to say, "Thank you to Denise, my friend," because she was the father of the baby. She claims rights to him, she does, because she was there through my whole pregnancy. She listened to me bitch about the pregnancy, I threw up on her—I mean, she was just there. She was excited and right from the beginning she was going to be the one that was going to help me have him. She supported me through this whole thing. And I think she had a blast when he was born too; she was my main coach. She was already crying the minute he was born, she was so happy. She should get some credit for this, because she felt like she was part of him, she was the daddy. She's so proud of him.

I just had a tubal ligation. It was very easy to decide. I had come through a whole pregnancy and given a baby up for adoption, so I better get a good form of birth control going, so I never have to go through that again. I wasn't going to make the same mistake twice. I had my two kids, and obviously all I wanted was my two kids or I would have kept my third. I didn't ever want to be put in that position again.

Update

MICHELLE AND HER two children live with her father and her grandmother. She cares for her grandmother, who is in failing health. John and Michelle are still married, but living apart, with no plans for reconciliation.

Comment

"WHO ARE THESE women?" ask all adoptive parents as they struggle to understand why a birthmother, this as-yet-unknown person, would give the gift of her child to them. Although they can range in age from fourteen to forty, a typical birthmother is eighteen to thirty years old. She is Caucasian, she has one or more children, and she has a high school diploma or a GED, although her educational accomplishments are rarely an accurate reflection of her intelligence. Birthmothers are often bright, articulate, and beautiful. Economic factors may lead to poor dental health and marginal living arrangements, but many of them work. Women who have already given birth tend to see the doctor less often than they should. Usually they are unmarried; if they are still married, it is likely to be to someone from whom they have been separated for several years but simply not bothered to divorce.

One of the most important things an adoptive family can do to benefit themselves and the birthmother during the adoption process is to try and understand her, without judgment, in the context of her own life. It helps the birthmother because out of this understanding comes empathy and compassion. This leads to generosity, in terms of time, attention, concern, and financial needs. It helps the adoptive parents because it brings smoother, more successful adoptions. Their heightened awareness helps them see potential problems more quickly, allowing them to avoid or solve them as soon as possible.

If adoptive parents could step back and look at adoption from the birthmother's point of view, the perspective might look something like this: She is six months pregnant, not feeling well, stuffed into her regular clothes because she can't afford maternity wear. She is unmarried, and the birthfather abandoned her after learning she was pregnant. She is supporting herself and raising her two-year-old son on welfare, which barely covers necessities, even with the addition of food stamps and gifts of government food surpluses. She has no transportation, goes nowhere, and feels completely trapped.

Her support system is so weak that there is no one she can ask to watch her son while she goes to the doctor, so she has not received prenatal care. Thinking she may want to place the child she is carrying for adoption, she looks in the yellow pages and talks to a complete stranger about this most personal decision. That person sends her five to ten adoption resumes of yet more strangers, who all say they want to adopt her child. According to their resumes they are all "financially secure, loving couples, living in safe neighborhoods with good schools." She picks one and waits for their call.

She talks to them, and they agree to meet. She wants to

meet in a public place, not only because she doesn't know them, but because she is embarrassed about her modest home. At their meeting she doesn't know what kinds of questions to ask, and decides to work with them because they "seemed really nice." She then talks to a lawyer for the first time in her life when their attorney calls. She may be informed that no home study or investigation has been done on the adoptive parents, and realizes that she has to trust them and their lawyer to tell her the truth and care about her interests.

The adoptive parents are fifteen to twenty-five years older than her, educated, experienced, well traveled, sophisticated, and sometimes use words she doesn't understand. Although the birthmother can barely support herself, they can support themselves and the new baby—and her for several months— and still have money left in savings. They own their home; she barely makes her rent each month. She is not represented by a lawyer; they are. Her friends marvel at her decision, wondering, How can she give her own baby away? She often asks herself this question, but is nearly certain that for her and her child to survive, she must do so.

Sometimes she is questioned so intensely by the social workers with whom she must meet that she thinks they are trying to talk her out of the adoption. This only adds to her confusion. When she begins to see a doctor, he treats her coldly, as do his nurses, when they learn of the planned adoption. Once she starts receiving financial assistance from the adoptive family, she loses her welfare payments. She worries that after the baby is born she won't be able to get back on it, or that welfare will make a mistake and there will be a delay in getting a check. What if she were to be evicted? She could never save up first and last months' rent and a security deposit for a new apartment. How would she feed her son? The adoptive parents can help her for only two months after the baby is born. She is frightened of the pain of labor, and worried that saying good-bye to the baby will be more than she can stand.

When an adoptive couple backs out of a planned adoption, they give little thought to the problems a birthmother like Michelle might face. The adoptive family believes the birthmother will easily find another family to adopt her child. This may very well be true, but there is no way to foresee the consequences of their action. Over the years I have seen adoptive parents change their mind about working with a birthmother because another child became available for them to adopt more quickly or inexpensively, because they became pregnant before a birthmother gave birth, or because they decided they couldn't accept something about a birthfather's background or availability. In every case the birthmothers were hurt, confused, and surprised, and in some cases they felt a deep sense of betrayal. More than one birthmother I've known has taken it as a "sign" that the family's change of heart meant that she was "supposed" to keep her baby. Adoptive parents are no more interchangeable to birthmothers than birthmothers are to adoptive families.

At those times when it seems the birthmother has all the control in an adoption, these facts must be remembered: An adoptive family may change their mind about the adoption during the pregnancy, after the baby is born, and during the period before the adoption is final. The birthmother who places her child in a two-parent household has no control if the adoptive parents later divorce, even if her primary purpose in placing her child was to have it raised by a mother and a father.

An adoptive family may even change their mind *after the adoption is final* and do what is called a readopt. A readopt occurs when a family adopts a child and then decides they no longer wish to have the child in their family and place it for adoption. The adoptive family is now acting as the birthfamily in seeking new parents for the child. This happens most often when a child is adopted from another country and has problems the family cannot or does not wish to cope with. A birthmother has no control over, and will not be informed of, a readopt.

All adoptive families ask the question, "If there is something wrong with this child, will we have to adopt it?" The simple answer is, "No, you don't." But this also means that if a birthmother's child is born with a medical problem, she may find herself and her child abandoned at the hospital. This is true even though the adoptive parents would have been forced to cope with the problem had they given birth to the child. I do not condemn these families for making the best choice for themselves. Part of educating preadoptive parents is helping them to recognize their boundaries; but part of that educational process is also getting them to understand that although they assume many risks in adoption, they have choices and power as well.

A misperception about birthmothers is that they are placing

their children for adoption because they don't care. I have found that it is just the opposite. Birthmothers care enough to place their child's welfare in a prominent position. It is not a completely selfless act, nor need it be. Birthmothers choose adoption because they see it as a way to create a better life, with more opportunities for their children *and* themselves. As contradictory as it may seem, many of them first try to have abortions, and are unable to do so, usually because they waited too long.

When I ask a birthmother to describe her ideal adoptive parents, she almost always answers, "A loving family that is financially stable." It is a broad, inclusive statement, and goes a long way toward explaining why birthmothers often choose single or gay parents to raise their children. The only bias I have seen is that birthmothers tend to want "Christian families." (Although at least half a dozen birthmothers have insisted this certainly did *not* include Catholics!) This preference exists because most of them were raised Christian and have little or no experience with Jews, Mormons, Moslems, or people of other religions.

When it came time to make one of the most important decisions of her life, Michelle made it thoughtfully and well. After experiencing the disappointment and hurt of being rejected by the first adoptive parents she chose, she rallied with a list of questions six pages long that she used to interview prospective families. The questions were intelligent and remarkably similar to those asked by the social service agencies that do the home studies of adoptive parents.

Michelle was more specific and methodical than most birthmothers. My experience is that choosing an adoptive family is frequently based on intuition; a birthmother reads the adoption resumes and "just knows." This is not to say she ignores the facts. A birthmother who is creative will be more drawn to a family that works in the creative professions. Similarly, birthmothers tend to choose families who look like her and the birthfather. Adoptive families are sometimes confused by this; they aren't sure if it is good news or bad news. It is good news in that not being young, beautiful, and rich carries no penalty, and bad news in that there is not much you can do but attempt to create an attractive, authentic adoption resume and wait to be chosen.

By the time adoptive parents come to see me to investigate the possibility of adoption, they have been through years of painful, expensive, and disappointing infertility treatments. They have been ready for years to be parents. Now that they realize that through adoption they are finally about to become parents, their pent-up anger and the frustration of infertility comes pouring out, aimed at adoption. "Why do I have to pay for this?" I am sometimes asked, a question I am sure was never posed to their fertility specialist. "Why do we have to meet her? Can't we just go to the hospital and pick the baby up or something?"

If there is one thought I would like adoptive parents to take away with them it is this: Remember always that it is the birthmother who will give them what no one else can, something they have spent years and much of their savings trying to achieve—parenthood and a child. If they simply go through the steps with patience, they *will* be parents.

A birthmother called me recently, just a month after giving birth. Her court-ordered spousal support check had never arrived, and she was unemployed. With much hesitation, she asked if it was possible to receive an extra month of financial support. I called the adoptive mom, expecting some resistance or resentment, but heard these words: "Of course! She gave me my happiness—how could I say no to her?" Those words have stayed with me: "She gave me my happiness." It is that simple truth that adoptive parents must remember through the demanding process of adoption, because that is what is at the end of this long, intense, sometimes costly road: a lifetime of happiness with a child.

7

Where Do Babies Come From?

BOBBI

A birthmother

**"When I got pregnant when I was sixteen, I wanted to
get pregnant because I wanted somebody to love."**

I'm twenty-two years old, born in Whittier Hospital on
Janine Street. That's how I got my middle name, Janine. I
love my mother for that one. My dad bought a home in
Riverside County; we moved there when I was eight and
that's when I started getting into trouble. The only thing in
our town was tract homes and the grocery store; there was
nothing to do. I started smoking when I was nine years old.
My dad used to smoke and I stole his. Who would suspect a
nine-year-old of stealing cigarettes? I didn't inhale, but I
learned.

I was sixteen when I started having sex. That's when I got
pregnant with Brittany. My first time, go figure—it would
have to be me, huh? But I was a late bloomer; all my friends

were already doing it. Arlene started when she was twelve, my best friend Jennifer was raped when she was thirteen. My dad told me, I get pregnant, I'm out of the house. My parents were watching as closely as they could watch, but sixteen years old, I'm going to do whatever I want to do.

My parents are very private people. They don't talk about their private life, their problems and stuff that they have in their family, and don't get involved with their children. They were not involved with absolutely anything that we did as children. When I had my miscarriage, my mom dropped me off at the hospital and she was gone. I had to find my own ride home.

She says that I abuse my daughter Brittany because I discipline her, which I have no choice because there's no father figure here for her, I'm the only one around. I spank her—I believe in spankings. I have a paddle specifically for Brittany; when she acts up, she gets the paddle. But according to my mom, I'm abusing her. She doesn't seem to remember me getting beat with a belt.

People think that I'm crazy when I say it, but I'm glad that my mom is the way she is. I don't know how to explain it, but like I can see it with my friend Jennifer. Jennifer's mom was always there hovering over her. She's always there for her, she's got a mom; she's got somebody she can depend on and she knows it. I don't; my parents don't help me. When I was homeless it was because of my parents—my parents kicked me out. I was homeless with two kids and my husband was beating me up every time I turned around. But if my parents were so sweet—you know, "Bobbi this," "Bobbi that"—I would have had them to lay against, I wouldn't have been able to do it myself. I would have always had help. Every time a problem came up, it's "Mama, help me." So I'm glad my mom is like she is because if she wasn't, I would not be this strong, I would not have the personality that I have.

When I got pregnant when I was sixteen, I wanted to get pregnant because I wanted somebody to love. My parents weren't there, all my friends were pregnant—I just wanted a baby. I guess it was just the thing to do. It's something I didn't want my parents to be involved in, but I had to tell them. I told my mother that I was pregnant. I had to say it three times because I was crying so hard. "Mama, I'm pregnant." My mom didn't say a word. Then she said, "You're going to have to tell your father." I said, "No, you tell him, I ain't telling him." A few weeks down the road she finally told my dad and my dad didn't talk to me for months. Not a hello, not a good-bye, not a "What are you doing?" not my name, nothing, for three months while we lived in the same house. When he finally did talk to me he told me, "Pack up and get out."

So I moved in with a girl named Lucy. I hardly knew her. She had a boyfriend who was a heroin addict, who moved in shortly after we did. I supported myself on welfare. Not long after that my boyfriend, Ray, got out of state prison.

He went to prison for receiving stolen property—him and his buddy stole a car. The sentence got dropped from a GTA [grand theft auto] to receiving stolen property. He went to Youth Authority first, then when he turned seventeen, he went to state prison, medium security. While he was there, he was the white man running the yard. They're segregated inside the cells—you know: blacks, Mexicans, whites—and they're also segregated into gangs. Ray's part of I.E.—Inland Empire. He told me that one of the guards told him that there was going to be a child molester released out into general population, instead of being in protective custody. They were going to release him into Ray's yard, and to "take care of him." So Ray took care of him by beating him almost to death.

Now I won't date anybody who's been in prison—I know what they're like. Their whole outlook on life is totally changed when they get out. They don't like cops, for one thing, they have very low self-esteem, and they don't think that they can make it in the world. They're all criminals! They do drugs; they think that crime is a way of life that you can't live life without. Ironically, most of them are really good to kids. Go figure. They don't think that criminal activity affects the kids. They do crime in front of them—they steal, they still do drugs. Even though they'd protect those children with their life, they don't think their criminal activity affects them. They're stupid. I don't think any of them have responsibility, because they go to prison and they're taken care of. They're given their schedule, they're fed their meals, they don't have to take responsibility for nothing but themselves. All they have to do is stay alive.

Anyway, I kicked Lucy and her boyfriend out and then me and Ray moved into our own apartment. We had a really good time—partied all the time, made a lot of friends, had a good time till things started to get serious. I wanted a relationship, a normal relationship; I was going on nineteen years old, and I had a little kid. So we started to fight.

I was pregnant again, but I didn't know it. This is when I got pregnant with the one I miscarried. Then Tonya, Miss Bitch, came back into the picture. Tonya and Ray were long-time friends—we've all known each other since elementary school. One day Ray comes to the apartment, says, "Guess who's here? It's Tonya!" I said, "Get her out of here. I don't like her, she knows it. She's only here to spite me. Get her out before there's a big fight." So he left with her and didn't come back until the next day, with hickeys from ear to ear. I found out that they had slept together, so I trashed the apartment.

A month and a day later he asked me to marry him. I thought he wasn't seeing Tonya no more, I thought that it was just that onetime thing. I was stupid. We got married a week later. I didn't find out until a few months ago that he spent part of our wedding night with Tonya, that tramp. They conceived a child that night. We got married one day and the next day I found out I was pregnant. We were happy together; he told everybody I'm pregnant, told everybody we got married. Tonya knew that we were pregnant at the same time. My kid would have been older.

He got arrested almost two weeks later for stealing a pizza from the delivery guy. He and his friends ordered a pizza to be delivered across the street. When it arrived, Ray ran out there and stole the pizza. The cops came and they were sitting there partying, the windows open, the music blaring as loud as it could be, eating pizza that they had just stolen. He got arrested, went to prison for two years in the toughest prison in California. It's his own dumb fault—he was still on parole.

I started to miscarry at his sentencing right after he got two years. I think it was stress—the doctor told me it was probably stress. I went to the hospital, had a miscarriage. I guess my heart was palpitating. I was in ICU for three days. Nobody was with me. My mom didn't care—remember I told you, my mom just dropped me off. My family went on vacation. I had to call looking for a ride when I got released.

Me and Ray got visitation in prison—they call it "Boneyards"; the legal term is conjugal visits. It's three days; you get permission to stay up there for three days with your husband inside this little apartment, inside the prison grounds. You have sex all day long, twenty-four/seven, sex day, sex night, sex morning, sex in the shower. The prison, by law, cannot take your marriage away from you, they cannot deny you access to your wife, or to your spouse. So they have conjugal visits only if you're married. We were married two weeks before, so, we got a Boneyard. That's when I got pregnant with Ashley, on a Boneyard.

We planned Ashley, because we talked about getting pregnant, and he wanted a kid. He didn't tell me about Tonya. He knew she was pregnant by then, and I think that's why he went along so enthusiastically about wanting a baby of our own, thinking, well, if I have a kid of his then our relationship can hold up. I think he did love me, but not all the way that I think love is supposed to be, but in his own distorted, demented, sick way. Not the way that I want to be loved, not even close.

When he got out he got a job working at AM-PM mini-market, but he robbed them—little by little at first, then he really robbed them. The cashiers have envelopes with their worker ID number on it. So when they get $100 in their cash register they need to envelope it and send it to the chute down to the vault for the bank. They call it cash drop. Ray would steal three or four of the other cashier's envelopes with the other person's numbers on them, replace them with Ray's envelopes with his number on it. So when the other cashier would drop those envelopes he would think that he's dropping his own, but actually he's dropping Ray's. Ray would steal the money that was in the other envelopes with the other guy's number on it.

Ray is bringing home $300 to $400 every few nights. Then he waited for the manager to turn around, took the manager's key, and robbed the vault, took about $4,000. He just closed it back up so it looked like the manager had done it. But the county's not stupid, county knows Ray's the only one working there that's on parole for theft to begin with. So they came to my house questioning me.

I told them that he didn't do it. They couldn't prove it; they had no fingerprints, nothing. That's why he didn't get busted, because there's no fingerprints. If I would have known then what I know now, I would have told the investigator, "Yeah, he did it, and here's some of the money." Because I had some of the money. But see, he didn't tell me that he robbed the vault. What he was doing was buying drugs with it. I didn't know he was using drugs. He used our rent money to buy a motorcycle and a car, so our rent didn't get paid. We were evicted.

I went back to my parents' home, he went back to his parents' home, he started doing drugs really heavy. I've been separated from him since that day. That's when I had had enough. Our daughter was just born, he's off buying cars, motorcycles, everything with our rent money, getting us evicted. I told him, "I'm leaving you. Good-bye." We haven't been together since.

So I went back to my dad's after being evicted, and we fight hellaciously when we live together. Plus, he didn't like Ray. I told him Ray's using drugs—I'm not going to hide the fact. So my dad forbade me to see Ray. I'm twenty years old, my dad forbade me to see my husband, so we know that didn't work out.

I had a doctor's appointment for both my kids to get their shots. There's no way I was going to deal with it myself. It's Ray's kid, Ray's responsibility too, so I went and picked him up. We're on our way home, my dad saw us in the car together. So when I got home, my dad asked me what the hell I was doing with him, and I said we had a doctor's appointment. "I thought I told you not to see him." I said, "You know what? He's my husband, you can't tell me not to see my own husband, I don't give a shit who you are." He's all, "Get out of my house." So I got out. And we were homeless, had nowhere to go.

That first night me and Ray pitched a tent for the kids. We went down into the woods and I stole my mom's tent. I stole money, I stole her gas card, I stole some food, I stole camping gear, I stole flashlights, batteries—I stole a lot from their house before I left. Welfare had just cut me off because Ray was working, so I didn't have money coming in.

The cops found us sleeping in the woods. They came up and asked me, "Why are you guys sleeping here?" I said, "Look, I'm homeless, I ain't got no place to go, this is where we're at for the night. My kids are sleeping, I'm not moving, take me to jail." He says, "No, just don't camp here tomorrow." So we didn't.

After that it was just me and the kids in the car, at a friend's house one night, at another friend's house another night, wherever we could. But basically, most of the time we were in the car, my Chevette. The backseats folded down so I could lay completely across the back end to sleep and, you know, the kids were small enough. From the time my youngest was three months old till the time she was five months old we were homeless. I was stealing food from the store, stealing diapers, formula. Finally, I applied for homeless aid and got some help from the county. They put us up in this little run-down motel for two weeks. But I didn't have any money for food, so I was still stealing food and diapers.

There's people that live worse than us—I know a lot of them. Brittany had fun; it was better than the car. I mean, it was a bed. Plus, I had got busted by the cops, they kept telling me if I sleep in the street again I'm going to take your kids. My mom was trying to get them away from me anyways. She called my social worker and she told my social worker I was homeless, living in the car with the two kids, that the county should take my kids.

After our time at the motel ran out I finally had to call my mom, after about three weeks of living in the car again, and tell her, "You gotta take my kids, I can't feed them." I was starving. I hadn't eaten in a week, I was living on water, if I could steal some bread . . . you know, bread and water. But Ashley was on formula, so it was getting hard to steal formula because the stores knew when I was coming in. And it was getting hard to feed Brittany because she's always hungry. It's hard to find handouts when you don't know that many people.

Finally, I got my first homeless check. They started me back on county, the 1st and the 15th checks. I used that money for phone calls, diapers, some food, things like that; I even bought cigarettes. I didn't have a cigarette the whole time—it was killing me. I had to make phone calls to try to find a place to live, and tell these people I'm homeless, if I move in the county was going to be paying my rent. There was only one place that would accept me, and that's where I moved to. That's when I met Frankie, and so that's how Taylor [the child Bobbi placed for adoption] was born.

He was standing outside my window because everybody kind of gathered around my window; my door was kind of the hangout place. I'd seen him before, I'd just never met him. I opened my door and I walked out and our eyes met and I just knew. I didn't even know his name, but I just knew that we were going to be together and sure enough we were. He stayed the night that night. We didn't do nothing, we just talked, we talked all night long. He wanted me to go out on a date with him Friday night. It was my first date. I was twenty-one years old—my first date. It was a big deal to me.

We never actually had sex. I can't believe it either, I'm so shocked, but there was never any intercourse. I actually waited five weeks, almost six, and he came over and we did sleep together and we did mess around a lot but we never actually had intercourse. There was no intercourse at all. He did come—I believe it was on my thigh, and from there they found their way up that little canal. I'm in a statistics book; the doctor wrote it down.

I figured I was pregnant, because I got deathly sick. I couldn't get off the couch, couldn't cook, couldn't take care of the kids, plus I missed a period. So I told him, "Go get a pregnancy test." He brought home two. I called Frankie into the bathroom and said, "Look, they're both pink." He didn't say nothing. I said, "Well, you're going to be a dad," and he still didn't say nothing. Then he kept telling me, "We can't have a kid, we can't have a kid, what are we going to do with a kid right now?" I said, "Well, it's a little too late now, you're already a father." He says, "No, I can't be." It was hard for him to comprehend.

He knew I was totally against abortion. We had talked before that if I was to ever get pregnant there's no way he'd allow me to have an abortion. Get that one—he wouldn't "allow" me to have one. He didn't want to contradict himself, make himself look like a dick. But he finally just gave in, just came out with what he really felt. He told me, "Look, go down tomorrow, have an abortion, I'll give you the three hundred dollars that it takes, I don't want to be a father right now." I started yelling at him. He said, "Don't yell at me. You haven't yelled at me for two months, don't yell at me now." I said, "Look, it's either I'm going to yell at you or I'm going to hit you. You take your pick." And he didn't say nothing. He just got his stuff and walked out the door. That was it.

He slept on the couch after that. I wouldn't allow him to sleep in the bed with me. He slept on the couch for two weeks until one day he decided he'd had enough. He grabbed all his things one morning and he was gone. I haven't seen him since. I hate him, because he can't take responsibility for his own child, he won't even acknowledge her. He still denies her.

I didn't have a conversation with him about the adoption. I called him and said, "My lawyer's going to be calling you." He didn't want any part of it, so he kept the decision mine. That's my child, not his. I knew I couldn't keep it. I could have—I'm not going to doubt my own abilities—I just didn't want to handle the stress. It's enough now to have to tell two kids they don't have a father. I wasn't going to do it again, I wasn't going to do that to Taylor.

I really didn't want to do adoption, because I didn't want to go through childbirth again. That was my only reason: I hate labor, I hate pain. Plus, I didn't know how I was going to react to actually giving my baby up. But I didn't want to have an abortion either, because once you do that there's no going back, there's no changing it. With adoption there is a change, I can change it. If I change my mind then I change my mind, that's my own problem.

I didn't get involved with the facilitator until I was absolutely positive I was going to give it up for adoption. She was real nice; she came right to my house. She brought me portfolios of prospective parents. I didn't like any of them but one. They lived in Wisconsin. She asked me if I wanted to go to Wisconsin to give birth. I said that would be fine as long as the accommodations suit me, my personal needs, what I want. I said, "If it's not what I want, then I'm not going to do it."

So at first these people agreed to everything I said, because they knew that if I didn't like it I wasn't going. Then they started changing as things went down the line. It went from, I was going to be there two months in advance, my own apartment, my food, my transportation, all my bills, my kids' diapers, doctors' bills, and I was going to live close to them. Then it went to, I was going to arrive two weeks before the baby was supposed to be born. They would pay for a month of my living; I'd be there two weeks after. They wanted my kids to stay with my mom while I went up there. They were going to move me into town, which was an hour away from them. They were not going to have me see a doctor, they wanted me to see a doctor here, then I would just go through the emergency room right when the baby was going to be born.

I felt like they were shopping at Pic and Save. I said to the facilitator, "You know what, drop them right now, drop them. I don't care to discuss it anymore, find me another couple now." And so, an hour later Phil and Amy called me. Amy was very straightforward, she didn't lie about nothing like the other couple did just to accommodate me. She said that her kids had passed away, and I didn't ask no questions. She said she didn't have much time to talk to me because she had to get my rent paid. So she went to the post office and mailed my rent right then and there.

She came out the next day and we just clicked. Amy's cool; she's just as weird as me. We're like best friends when we're together—we talk about other people, we gossip, we like and dislike the same things. We can bitch about the exact same things. Phil's cool. I don't know him that well, but for somebody to stand by their wife through the death of two children and go through the adoption and everything and they are still together goes beyond questioning. My husband leaves me, beats me up, does drugs on the birth of one child—a healthy one at that.

It felt funny when they left the hospital with her—I felt like they were leaving with my child. But it's not like I knew it wasn't coming. I saw Amy and the baby just three days ago. It felt weird, but didn't feel as funny as when they were taking her from me at the hospital. I felt more that she was Amy's child three days ago than I did when they actually left the hospital. I was sitting there holding her; I knew that I had given birth to her and I knew that she wouldn't be there if it wasn't for me. But at the same time I felt, That's Amy's child.

The high point in adoption is there is no abortion, the child's still alive. For me, the most satisfying part of it was I was giving Phil and Amy a baby that they would never be able to have by themselves. I was the most important thing in their lives so far. If it wasn't for me they wouldn't have a child—I mean, they would, but they wouldn't have Taylor. The low point of adoption is, that's your child. You've given birth to your child, it's yours, nobody else's, and you're giving it to somebody to raise that has no blood relation to that child at all. If I could have kept Taylor, I would have kept her. I'm not going to deny that to spare Phil and Amy's feelings. But it's unfair to her not to have a father. It's unfair to her to be raised on welfare, it's unfair to her to have two other siblings without a father and have to go through the same emotional bullshit they're going through right now.

Brittany doesn't have a dad, and I see the effect it has on her. The kids go to school and it's, "Oh, my daddy did this, and my daddy did that, and my daddy, my daddy, my daddy." All she has is, "My daddy's in prison." And that's the only thing that Ashley's going to have too: "My daddy's in prison, my daddy does drugs, my daddy didn't want me." It's bullshit to have to put another child through that. And keeping Taylor, it would have been just as much of a struggle, more, for me to go through school and get their lives stable and on track as possible. It would have been three times as hard.

I'd change the whole legal aspect of adoption. I believe you should be able to advertise for a birthmom; I think that it should be a law that birthmoms go through counseling. I went to counseling, and Lord knows I don't talk about my personal life. I think first-time moms should not decide on adoption until after the baby's born. If Taylor was my first child, I'm sorry, but Phil and Amy wouldn't have her. Because once you go through the labor, the birth, the pain of going through it, the holding of your child, it becomes real, there's really a baby there. And for first-time moms it's an experience that cannot be explained. They know that they're pregnant and they know that there's going to be a baby but they don't know the feeling until after birth. If I was an adoptive parent I wouldn't like a child from a first-time mom.

I don't think social workers should play a part in adoption. The one at the hospital was cool. He came in, he said, "Is this what you want to do?" I said, "Yes," he said, "OK, sign the paper." I can see if I hesitated with the word "yes" he'd have some questions. But the county social worker created a problem for me. She told me she didn't think I was really ready. She said I seemed sort of tense and unfocused about the whole adoption. She doesn't know me. Her outlook on my attitude, my personality, and my feelings toward the adoption were so wrong. All she was was an interference in the whole thing. I think that the lawyer should get the papers signed and get it over with. I don't think the social worker should be there at all.

My future goal is I'm going to have a career. I'm going to make as much money as I want to make doing what I want to do and voicing my opinion however I want to voice it. I'm not going to have a boss, I'm not going to have somebody tell me I can and cannot do whatever I want to do. I'm going to have a career where I can give my children everything that they want.

As soon as I get my paperwork and everything in, I'm going to take psychology classes. It's a career that I'd be good at because I know people so well. You know that saying, "Take the one thing that you're good at and make a career out of it." Well, I can judge people pretty much a hundred percent right on. Every once in a while, like Ray, every once in a while I screw up. Ray's my only major fuckup. But otherwise I pretty much get it right on, about the attitudes of people and how they are and whether or not you can trust them or not. I wanted to be a lawyer, but . . . I might get there some-day, I might be both. What kind of better lawyer than one that took psychology?

Update

AFTER RAY'S RELEASE from prison, he and Bobbi lived together for a while and had a son. Ray is now back in prison. Bobbi has purchased a mobile home and is taking a two-year course of study to become a respiratory therapist. Genetic testing showed that Ray was not the father of Tonya's child.

Comment

AS BOBBI BEGAN to talk about her first steps toward an adop-tion, she said, without elaboration, "I didn't get involved with the facilitator until I was absolutely positive I was going to give it up for adoption." What is a facilitator? The question addresses one of the most important parts of an adoption. A facilitator is a person who finds the birthmother for the adop-tive family. Most accurately, she is an adoption advertising service.

To understand why adoptive parents would consider hiring a facilitator we have to step back and see what kinds of op-tions are available to them in their search for a birthmother. It's a short list. Sending out hundreds of adoption resumes to clinics, doctors, and hospitals worked well in years past, but is rarely effective now. Thirty-two states allow adoptive parents to advertise the fact that they are searching for a birthmother and a child to adopt. These ads appear under "Adoption" in the classified sections of major city newspapers and national publications like *USA Today*. A typical ad will read, "Active, loving, financially secure family longs to adopt newborn. Call John and Terry anytime." Birthmothers respond to the ads and speak directly to the adoptive families. But most families do not want to do the advertising themselves because they feel vulnerable, and because they cannot be available twenty-four hours a day to answer calls. So although this method is still effective, it too is becoming outmoded.

A few enterprising individuals, mostly adoptive mothers who had been through the process themselves, saw the need to help birthmothers and adoptive parents find one another, and created the facilitation business. This is how it works. After a family has hired an adoption attorney and created an adoption biography with photos, called an "adoption resume" or "birthmother letter," they hire a facilitator. A typical facilitator's fee is $6,000-plus. The facilitator spends several thousand dollars each month advertising in yellow pages throughout the state or the country, with ads that say something like, "Pregnant? Considering adoption? Call 1-800-FOR-HELP. Medical and living expenses paid as legal." Pregnant women call the facilitators, who make sure a person, and not a machine, answers the phone twenty-four hours a day, seven days a week. The facilitator obtains background information on the birthmother, a verification of pregnancy, and sends her five to ten adoption resumes so that she may choose the family she wants to adopt her child. If she doesn't like any of those families, the facilitator will send her more resumes until she finds one she does like. (To send more than ten or so at once usually only overwhelms a birthmother and makes her choice more difficult.)

For most facilitators, the job is over once the match is made. But many remain in contact until after the birth, assisting with emergencies and referrals for doctors and housing. If the adoption does not go forward because the birthmother changes her mind, most facilitators will find another birthmother for the family until there is a successful placement. This last point is very important; I warn my clients to make sure that the onetime fee insures the facilitator's efforts until an adoption is secure.

All facilitators are not created equal, and abuses do occur. Some facilitators try to pressure adoptive parents into accepting a birthmother with whom they are uncomfortable, whose expenses they cannot afford, or whose baggage includes potential birthfather problems they find too risky. Others try to shame them by asking questions like, "Do you want a baby or not? If you want a perfect baby, forget it, don't waste my time." I have seen facilitators drop adoptive families—after being paid in full—and refuse to work further for them because they think the family is being too "fussy." I have been part of an adoption where the facilitator was possessive of the birthmother, filling out her questionnaire forms for her. In answer to simple questions such as "What are your future goals?" she wrote again and again, "None of your business." We were fortunate that a successful adoption occurred in spite of her antagonism.

For these and other reasons—resistance to change; a loss of part of their role—many adoption attorneys are reluctant to work with facilitators. Adoption attorneys used to locate the majority of birthmothers; but they cannot compete with facilitators unless they spend the same amount of money and take the time necessary to perform the same tasks, then pass the cost on to their clients. Using a facilitator increases the cost of adoption, but so does individual advertising, and the money is spent on the all-important foundation of every adoption—finding a birthmother and a child to adopt.

Many people have expressed their discomfort with adoption advertising, whether it is by the adoptive parents or a facilitator, finding it unseemly for so intimate an event. They ask, "Isn't there some other way we can all find one another?" Although many have considered the question, no one has as yet discovered a better alternative. The Internet may prove to be a valuable resource in the future, but a disappointingly small number of birthmothers are now located in that way. It may be that the very thing that makes the Internet so wonderful—its global range—is what birthmothers least want in an adoption. They prefer to speak to a person and know that within twenty-four hours they will be able to meet a facilitator or an adoptive family in person.

California is one of fewer than twenty states that has outlawed any type of adoption advertising by adoptive parents. This means they must either hire a facilitator or advertise out of state. I advocate not only for the legalization of adoption advertising in all states, but also for the most open and readily available type of advertising, including television and radio, so that any birthmother, no matter how isolated and frightened, will know there is a place where she can turn. There is no reason to be delicate, no decency to be protected, by making it hard for a birthmother to find an adoptive family when she is in crisis. If she could look in a local newspaper or watch a TV program that would help her locate someone quickly, it would allow her to receive the prenatal care she has been unable to afford, assure her of an adequate supply of food, or simply put her mind to rest about her pressing problem. Bobbi is a perfect example; she lived in a rural area and had two children, no child care, and no car. Within an hour of making a phone call she had someone at her door to help her.

Open advertising can help the "prom moms" and other women who give birth in panic or despair and throw their babies away. In Los Angeles County alone there are approximately two dozen "trash can babies" found each year, most of whom do not survive. Adoptive parents, because they are generally mature and financially stable, are aware of the steps to take to inform themselves about adoption law and procedure. Birthmothers are younger and less sophisticated, and every effort must be made to see that they can find adoption resources as easily and as quickly as possible.

THE FOLLOWING IS a poem written by Bobbi to the daughter she placed for adoption, Taylor Rose.

Miracles

God blessed me with a child once, though young and still unwed. He placed her safely in my womb, as I laid there in his bed.

God blessed me with a child twice, he must have heard my prayer. He gave a man and his wife a baby girl to share.

Time went by, day-by-day, our baby's three month's old. Once in love, but now divorced from all the lies he told.

Alone again, now raising two, I try to do my best. I pray to God for strength each night, before I lay to rest.

A year has passed, we're doing fine, God keeps us in his sight. He's helped me through the stress it takes to try and raise them right.

The Lord gave me life on purpose with some intent in mind. Through all those years in question, only later would I find.

God had a prayer to answer, one that truly deserved to be. God needed someone special. God finally needed me.

I only saw him once, but once was all it took. I knew from then we would be one, he had that certain look.

The chemistry was spooky, our eyes spoke sounds unheard. We could have said a thousand things without a single word.

Good-bye was all he said to me, good luck and see you soon. He's leaving his own child, that grows within my womb.

I know there is a reason why this child was conceived. Please help me find the answer, Lord, please help me to perceive.

God blessed me with your child once, she's the answer to

your prayers. God blessed me with this miracle and told me I should share.

So I give to you my miracle, the greatest gift that's known. A chance to share your faith and love, with a child of your own.

Please treasure her existence, and praise her every move. Always give her encouragement, when she discovers something new.

A chance to be her parents, and watch her as she grows. A chance to be responsible for all the things she knows.

You'll be there for her firsts in life, her steps, her words, her goals. And you'll be the one she counts on to nurse her through her colds.

You'll be there when she asks for help, or needs you just to talk. You'll be the only one to hold the key, that fits her secret lock.

You'll be the one to catch her tears for every time she cries. You'll be the one to answer all her hows and whys.

God has made a miracle, complete with lace and bows.

Heaven sent an angel down to give us Taylor Rose.

8

Childless Mother, Motherless Child

JANE

A birthmother

"Seven kids, five up for adoption. There's a certain
instinct that comes along with being a mother, and I
don't have it."

I'm adopted. Nancy, who is my adoptive mom, worked
with my birthmother, Denise. She knew Denise was an alcoholic, because she would come into work drunk, and was
getting a divorce from her husband, who is supposedly my
birthfather. Denise came in one day and said, "Well, I've
proved paternity in my divorce case, and I don't need Jane
anymore, so I'm going to be putting her in a foster home."
My adoptive mom, Nancy, wasn't able to have kids; she said,
"Don't do that, I'll take her." Denise said, "Well, you better
come tonight and get her." Because she's real cold, like how
I am.

My adoptive parents went over there to get me and I had

cradle cap so bad they had to shave my head. The back of my head is flat from permanently lying on my back. They said I wasn't sitting up; nine months old, I should be sitting up. But nobody's attending to me and helping me to do that. I had marks on my ankles and on my wrists because she'd go out at night and drink, so she would just tie me to the crib with one of my limbs so that I wouldn't climb out of the crib, and just tell the lady that lived below, "Maybe you can listen for her." So I spent a lot of time alone. She never really cared for me.

At first my dad said, "Nancy, we're not getting along, and I don't think it's a good idea for us to adopt a child." And she said, "I don't care what happens from here on out. Jane's not going back to be with her. I'm never giving her back. Look at the spot that she's in."

Denise came back around when I was about two years old. She'd been arrested for drunk driving. My dad went to go get her, he bailed her out, and they put up their house. She jumps bail, and they lost their house. So now my dad says, "We don't want to help you find her. She didn't want you. Now damn it, why do you keep on asking about this woman for? Why do you want to go and disrespect Nancy when she loved you?" And I say, "Because I just feel like something's not right. I feel like I'm out of place, something's wrong. I feel like someone's lying to me." I have a big problem with that. I always think everybody's lying to me. I don't trust nobody.

I said to my dad, "You're a cop. You could run any name you want on that DMV computer—go in there and run it."

He said, "She didn't want you. What if I do bring up the address, what do you expect to happen if you find her?" "I'm not sure how I might act. What would I say to her? I would probably beat her to a pulp." He said, "That's exactly the reason why I'm not going to be trying to find an address." I said, "I want to know what she looks like." He said, "Take a look in the mirror."

At one point Denise contacted Nancy and said, "Well, Jane should be graduating high school by now." Nancy told her, "She graduated last year, and she's in a mess of a life, and I don't really have time to go over it with you." Denise said, "That's not really what I called for anyway. I was hoping I could borrow some money." I don't know what has happened to her. She probably drank herself to death. I hope. I should probably try to find my birthfather. He told my adoptive parents at the court hearing for adopting me, "I'll do whatever, because that child don't need to be with her. She's whacked."

I would prefer the truth is what I think it is: that I'm the product of an affair. I think my adoptive dad was having an affair on Nancy with Denise. He has cheated—that's how he met my stepmom, so I know he's done it once. I think that I was the product of an affair, and that he came clean with Nancy and said, "Hey, I've had an offspring, let's go and get her, because the woman I had her with is kind of crazy." I told him this straight to his face, and he just said, "You've got a hell of an imagination, girlfriend."

They adopted me when I was nine months old, got divorced when I was two, and then I went back and forth between them. I stayed at my dad's for the school year, then I'd be with my mom for the summer.

My dad remarried, and Loretta, my stepmom, got pregnant when I was ten years old. That's when I found out I was adopted. Nancy went off on my dad, "What the hell do you mean, 'Loretta's pregnant'? How could Loretta be pregnant? You have a low sperm count—we had to adopt Jane."

Out of spite for my dad she starts immediately like scolding me, but telling me, "Yeah, didn't you know you were adopted?" I can still remember her leaning down at my level, "Don't you know? Didn't you know? I thought you knew. That's why you don't look like none of us." Nobody told me. To this day I get mad. Nancy said, "I always told you." And I said, "You're a goddamn liar, because I would have remembered."

Nancy said, "I've decided you're going to live with your dad now that you're going to be having a new brother or sister." Now that I'm an adult I know that what she was really saying was, "I'm sending you to L.A. to go mess up your dad's new life." And I did.

My beginning complaint with Loretta was that she was re-creating another life with my dad that was real. See, I wasn't real. So I resented her because I knew that as long as she was around I was no longer number one. I was the "helper"— that's what Loretta used to call me. "She's a good helper, she's a good helper." When she got pregnant with my sister I said, "I hope your baby dies." But that's only because I was distraught, I didn't understand what was happening.

My dad wouldn't allow me to go nowhere and do nothing—never got to be with no kids, never had no friends, couldn't do after-school projects or activities. He said, "What if something happens?" I can't use the phone because I'm not allowed to have phone calls. "For what," my dad would say, "what do you need to talk about?" It was too much; you've got to teach your kids to discipline *themselves*. Because when I'm finally fourteen and got a little taste of what's going on, look what happened.

I started ditching school. I had these two identical twin friends, Tami and Teri; they were the hos of the town. So I immediately latched on, I said, "Yeah, I gotta get with them!" Their mom was a single mom, so she was gone all the time. They lived right by the school, so we could easily ditch and go to their house and hang out all day. They had water beds; they were allowed to smoke cigarettes. By this time I'm in the ninth grade, and running away frequently. I'm running away every Friday, and I'm saying to Tami and Teri, "Hey, do you mind if I stay here for the weekend?" They said, "No, we don't care."

I was fourteen years old when I met Al. We were caught having sex in my dad's bed. I'd never even had a period yet, that's how fresh I was. My dad said to his parents, "You know I can have your son arrested, twenty-one years old, my daughter's fourteen. And now there's blood in my bed, there's blood in my bed!" So my dad said, "I don't want you to see him anymore." I remember it was near Valentine's Day and I was walking with my dad at the mall, and I went to grab his hand and he said, "You're an adult now. You do adult things—you don't grab my hand in the mall." It made me feel like I was dirty, that I'd done something bad. From then on it went downhill.

Al was the only person paying attention to me; he never told me no. I could say and do whatever I want, and he pretty much was going to say, "OK." Al was smoking cocaine, but I didn't know what cocaine was then. I didn't realize that he was heavily involved in it, but my dad evidently knew. My dad never told me, "He's a drug dealer." He just said, "He's a bad guy." I didn't know—what's a "bad guy"? He was paying attention to me, he didn't seem like a bad guy to me.

I started stealing from my dad. I'd steal money, I would steal things from my dad that I thought Al wanted, things that we could use, like cameras. I stole some perfume from my stepmom that I knew my dad liked on her, because I wanted Al to smell it on me. My dad put up with about three months of me actually sneaking out and seeing Al and catching me. Then he just said, "You don't live here anymore. You don't live here anymore. Don't come back here, because you don't want to be here, because you keep running away from here. These are the rules, so if you don't want to follow these rules then you don't live here." I couldn't believe my ears.

My dad gave full custody of me to Al; he became my legal guardian. I was fourteen years old. My dad said, "I'm done with her, OK? She don't want to live here, she wants to be with him, so he can have her." The judge said, "What's going on? You're her father, you're not supposed to be doing this." And he said, "She doesn't want to be with us in our family, and I have another daughter, and I'm not going to expose my other daughter to her popping in and out whenever she feels like it, running away, and causing the family to be in total chaos. I'm not going to do it."

My dad was responsible for a certain amount of money every month that was given to Al's mom and dad because we lived at their house. Al was directly responsible for making sure that I went to school, and I did what I was supposed to do, and I didn't get in trouble. I lived in the house; Al lived behind the garage in a greenhouse that was converted into a bedroom, but he always ended up being in my room. Al and I were fighting and coming in and out at all hours, and his mom and dad said, "You know what, we know you have sex, and you're not supposed to be having sex, we told you that from the start. If you want to do that, then you need to go somewhere else."

Al was a trash truck driver when I first met him, and he would go to San Pedro, and he realized he was picking up cocaine in the Dumpster for his boss. When he figured out his boss was running drugs he robbed his boss's house. He climbed underneath the house, came up through his closet, and stole a safe. We took the safe back to our house; we blew it up. In the safe was fifteen pounds of all the pills you could ever imagine in this big Ziploc bag, and money, a gun, drugs, a scale, pictures of family, birth certificates, and other stuff.

Al was afraid of the gun, so he threw it off a bridge. When the tide went out the police found the gun, and linked it back to Al and me. I had a bank account and Al put all the stolen money in my name, $175,000, knowing that I'm a minor and they're not going to get me.

One day Al said, "Before you go to the beach I want you

to go to the store and buy the usual stuff [for smoking cocaine]." I knew that as soon as I got him the stuff that I can leave for the day. I went to the store, I ran in the bedroom, threw the stuff on the bed, and I heard, "Click, click." I looked up and there's a gun there and a man said, "Don't move." The cops raided our house. I was sixteen. They wanted to let me go because they knew Al was responsible, but my fingerprints were on everything, the money was in my name.

Grand larceny, that's what I got in trouble for in the end. They wanted to know where did the money come from. I said, "Well, I've been working at Taco Bell." I didn't realize how much money that was. I served nine months in probation camp for Al.

They contacted my dad afterward and said, "Hey, Al's been her legal guardian and it's not working out, because look, she got in trouble." The probation officer said, "She's going to be getting out pretty soon and we want her to live with you. She's seventeen now, and she's only got one year till she's eighteen. We don't want her to be with Al." My dad said, "All right, I'll take her back in."

He picked me up from juvenile probation camp, took me home, and said, "OK, these are the rules: No Al here. I know you're going to see him, but not here. You don't live in the house, you live in the trailer on the property." I have to eat in the house, and I'm to shower in the house, but I can only come in when I'm invited, I can only come in when someone's there. I don't have a key, I can't use the phone, and I have to have a job in two weeks, or school. I had to be home at a certain hour—you know I wasn't doing that. So I would come home, my dad would have locked the trailer door so I couldn't get in. Then I started staying at Al's, and my dad started reporting it to my probation officer. So, finally I just made a deal with my probation officer, it's like, "I'm just not going to live at my dad's. It just didn't work out." Then my granddaddy died and left me $10,000.

Soon as I turned eighteen I got the money, and I got pregnant. We spent all that money on cocaine. I smoked cocaine the whole time I was pregnant with Travis. I smoked $10,000 worth and then some, with Al. I'd been writing checks everywhere, all around my city; I had a check guarantee card because I had $10,000 in an account. But I began to write bad checks and got arrested, and I had Travis in jail. And that sucked because I was handcuffed to the bed.

It was my first baby, and they don't care when you go into labor and you're in jail. They checked me and they say, "Yes, you're in labor, but it's going to be a long time. Sit down on that hard bench right there and start timing your own contractions. Don't move and don't talk to nobody."

They don't call the ambulance to come get you at the jail until it's going to be almost time, because they don't want to waste their time taking you over to L.A. County General Hospital if you're not gonna have the baby right then. It costs money for them because I'm an inmate. So I delivered downstairs in the emergency room, because they waited till the last minute. They're telling me, "Bear down, and push," you know. And I don't know what "bear down, push" is, I'm eighteen years old, I don't know.

They sent a cop from the men's jail with me, because there

was no female. The doctor's telling the cop, "She's going to rip because she's pushing so hard. If you would uncuff one of her arms that would give her some leverage so she could bear down." And he goes, "I'm not doing that because we're on the ground floor." The doctor's like, "She's not going to take off!" I ripped all the way through.

So I had the baby. I was chained to the bed, the bed was cemented into the floor. The chain went around my ankle, and then there was a master lock that would allow me to go as far as the bathroom, and then to my door, which was kept locked at all times. The social worker came and said, "You gotta make a big decision. I can't let you use the phone, but I need you to tell me who's going to come get your baby. And whoever you tell me, and sign this paper, that's who's got to come, and if they don't come within three days, then the child goes to Children's Services."

I told him I wanted my dad to come and get him. When I got back to jail the next day I called my dad; he still hadn't picked him up. He was telling me that Loretta's mom had died, and he didn't know if he was going to be able to go get the baby because my stepmom was in dire straits, and making funeral arrangements. "Loretta's in no condition to be taking care of your baby." She was cussing at me on the other line, saying, "How dare you call here and expect something. My mom just died." I told her, "Get off the phone, I'm talking to my dad. I didn't call for you—mind your own business."

But he came and got Travis, and I served my time, and when I came out Travis was a year old. He didn't know who I was. Me and Al got an apartment and went to my dad's house to get him. Loretta was heartbroken the day I came and said, "I want my kid." I kept him for about three days, because he just wanted Loretta. He just constantly cried for "Ra-Ra." So I took him back over there and gave him back to them. "Here, have him. He doesn't want me." My dad goes, "This can never happen again. You can never come and get him and take him back and bring him back. I won't have it; it's not fair."

Now I think my dad was saying it was more responsibility than I was willing to do. But see, I was too young then, I couldn't figure that out. So I thought, I gotta have another kid. So I immediately got pregnant with Alex.

Things were pretty normal. I wasn't going to jail, and we weren't stealing. We were doing a little bit of speed, but not really. We had our own apartment, and Al was working and things seemed to be OK. I thought, Well, Alex is it. I'm not ever giving this one up. Alex has been through the mill with me—seen me go to jail, slept in a car with me. He's stolen with me. I'd tell him, "Put this in my purse." We went through the whole Children's Services thing; he's a trouper.

Every child I had after Alex, I gave up. Seven kids, five up for adoption. There's a certain instinct that comes along with being a mother, and I don't have it. I got a kid for every year: three, four, five, six, seven, eight, and Travis is ten. Travis lives with my dad, and Alex lives with Al. I'm ashamed because of that, even today, because I was lazy. I was lazy, because after you have a baby you don't need to get pregnant right away after, and that's what started happening. I'd have a baby, I would go home from the hospital, and you're not supposed to have sex for six weeks. Al would say, "Uh-huh, you need to be giving me some of, you know," and I would get pregnant. Now why couldn't I just say, "I'm going to get the pill." I never would go to my follow-up appointments, and I would get pregnant. That's laziness.

Why would I feel the need to reproduce so many damn times when I know it hurts to have a baby? When you get pregnant and you have a baby, that doesn't necessarily qualify you as a mother. I don't have the instinct. As I started getting pregnant with the other ones, it just seemed to be an inopportune time. The real truth is, I did so many drugs I could never bring myself to go and have an abortion because I was afraid if they put me to sleep I would die.

The first time I got pregnant and I gave the baby up I was far along. It was only three weeks after I met the lawyer that I had the baby. By then we were living in a motel, living off welfare and just scraping and stealing and getting by. I was big pregnant and didn't want to keep the baby because I knew I couldn't take care of it. I looked in the phone book under "Adoption" and got ahold of an attorney. My original plan was to make the people think they were going to get the baby and then at the last minute I was going to say that I couldn't do it. I wanted to do that because I told Al, "We need money, we need money, and this is the only way I can think of to get money," because he wasn't working. I didn't know what I wanted to do, but I knew I needed money. So I was going to do that.

I met them two times. The first time they met me they took us out to dinner with the lawyer. That's when I made my final decision, the first time I met them. I said, "Yeah, go ahead and let them have him." I went into labor seven days later. I didn't even know them. She was a bitch to me, she treated me terribly. Afterward I said I wanted some photographs and they said they didn't want to give me photographs because I tested positive, and the baby tested positive for speed. I told the lawyer I was going to sue them, so he gave me some. Then they just wrote me some real nasty letters, real short, "Here's the pictures you wanted. There's no reason for you to be asking for pictures or anything like that, he's just fine considering what you done to him while he was inside your womb." It just seemed like such a hassle, I let it pass. I just let the whole thing go.

Then I got pregnant again, and those people [the new set of adoptive parents] gave me lots of money over the months. The lady was really good to me. They bought clothes for Alex and she came every month and took me to the doctor. She was there when the baby was born. That was a girl. I really felt sorry for the woman that I gave the kid to, and they were just really kind to me. I called them a few months after the baby's born and said, "Al went to jail, and me and Alex don't got nowhere to live." So they gave me a thousand dollars.

When Al got out of jail his job took him back, but they said, "You have to relocate because that's where we got work for you." So we packed up and moved. Al said that he knew going up there that there was bad things going on in that area. He knew that, but he never wanted to tell me. We got evicted a whole bunch of times, so I found out about squatting.

I found a vacant house, went over there, broke in, changed the locks, made a rental agreement, forged the name, and lived there for four and a half years. Well, our house, because it was a squatter house, was tagged. That's how we got involved with Vincent, because he had tagged the house, which means he takes proceeds from whatever goes on in that house. He lived a few houses down from us, and he lived on that block his whole life, and knew what we were doing there. Since we were living there illegally and doing illegal stuff, Vincent knew we weren't going to call the cops on him if he broke into our house. So Vincent started breaking in and stealing stuff. He said to Al, "I'm taxing you for being on my block and selling drugs, and I need to get a portion. If you make a hundred dollars a day, I want forty of it." He had houses all over for that. He was involved with the Vagos, which is a gang, people who make drugs. He had "Public Enemy #1" tattooed on his stomach.

One day Vincent said, "I don't want nothing in your garage, I want to have your wife." So I would be with Vincent Thursday, Friday, Saturday, and part of Sunday, and I would be with Al and Alex the rest of Sunday, Monday, Tuesday, and Wednesday.

I'd have babies and give them up, and have babies and give them up, and that went on all during that time. One day Vincent said, "You don't understand. I'm not with you 'cause I'm loving you, I'm with you 'cause . . ." And Al was standing there, and he said, "Hey, shhhhh." Well, Vincent wasn't keeping that quiet. "You've been traded for drugs. Don't you know that? The past two years have been nothing but a trade. How do you think you guys stay in drugs all the time? How come you think nobody comes and taxes you guys? Because I've been protecting you." I looked at Al; I had tears coming down my face. I said, "You tricked me." I wasn't mad at Vincent; it wasn't Vincent's fault. I was getting mad more at myself because I trusted Al all that time. "You couldn't even have told me you traded me for drugs? You don't trust me?"

I thought Vincent cared about me. You don't have sex with somebody for almost three years and don't think they don't care. Vincent stopped Al from hitting me. I signed my name right here across Vincent's heart and they tattooed it right where I signed it. He lived a very reckless life. He's probably dead by now.

I was mad because Al told me we weren't making money selling drugs, and I knew that we were, but I could never find the money. One day I was cleaning and I was standing on the counter, and there was a cookie jar high up in the cabinet. I pulled the cookie jar down and there was $2,700 in there.

I didn't tell Al that I found the money because I was so pissed. Because I would ask him for things like, "Can I buy tampons, please, I'm bleeding, I need tampons." And he would say, "Go steal them." I knew that we had money, and why should I steal them unless we have to. Only steal if I have to, right? Because it's a risk. "No, you steal when I tell you to steal."

When I found the money I called Vincent up and said, "Meet me at the airport, we're going to Vegas." We left Thursday, came home Monday. When I came home Al had obviously figured out what I'd done. Soon as I turned the key and opened the door, he hit me and broke my nose. I immediately started choking on my blood. I was holding Alex's hand; he was only four. Alex was just splattered with blood, all over. I told him, "Call 911." I started going to the car and Al said, "You ain't going nowhere." He broke my collarbone so that I couldn't drive.

When the cops came, Al said he didn't know how I got like that. He told them, "She stole twenty-seven hundred dollars from the family and went to Vegas with her boyfriend." They're looking at Al and they're going, "We know what's going on at this house. We're not stupid, OK? Don't start off by telling us 'she stole twenty-seven hundred dollars'; you all are dope fiends, and that's what's going on here. Did you do this?" Al said, "I don't know what happened. She took money, and I was mad, and I heard her car pull up and she was coming in the front door, and I saw red, and I could have done that to her." They said, "You got blood all over you— obviously you did this." Al was out in seventy-two hours.

Al put a lot of pressure on me to steal. It was my responsibility to make sure that we always had what we needed. It was my responsibility to make sure that all the squatting was done correctly so that we had a roof. Al would make things hard for me if he didn't have something to eat, and if we didn't have enough money I had to go steal whatever we needed because I had a purse. It was his job to drive the van and run interference in the store.

It didn't always work. I used to get caught once a year. But I was glad when I got caught because then I knew that I was good for another year. If you get caught once a year if you're stealing every day, that's good odds. So I knew that when I went to jail I'd get a little rest, sleep for a while, get a little fat on me, come out, and do it again.

Things were getting bad; Al was beating me all the time. I wasn't able to go to any stores without them recognizing who I was and following me around. We'd run our time out there, and things were thin. I remember sitting on the bathroom floor and just saying, "You're not going to have anything better, this is it. Don't even want for anything else, just accept what you've got and go on, and be happy if you get something better."

We'd been going into Wal-Mart and picking the lock where they have like the expensive cameras on the bottom. Al would go in and pick the lock, and I would go in and sweep it, because it's better to have a two-man operation. One time he came out too quick, and I said, "What happened?" And he's like, "It was unlocked." I said, "I'm not going in there. They're waiting for us." And I knew it, because I'd stolen so much that I could feel it, right here. I said, "I'm not going in." He said, "You are." I'd always trusted him, and I didn't think he would set me up to take a fall on purpose.

When it was unlocked we should have left, because as soon as I stepped out of the store they grabbed me, and Al drove off. I was so sick of everything that I told the cops, "Take me to my house, and I'm going to show you where there's stolen stuff. I'm done, finished. This is it. It's just ended." Every time I came out of jail I went right back and did the same thing. I knew that if I destroyed where I lived I would be done there.

I took them to my house and Al was hiding in the loft in

the garage. I was such a good little speed freak that I had kept all these records, I had a folder of all these receipts, and I said, "Here you go," just mapped it out. Al fell through the loft while we were in the garage. I knew he was in there because he kept setting off the car alarm. They arrested me, they arrested Al, they confiscated everything in our house, and we both went to jail. Alex stayed with my dad. They prosecuted me for grand theft; I spent seven months in the women's prison.

This was exactly the time I was pregnant with Ben, my last one, when I got busted at Wal-Mart. Every time I went to jail I would be pregnant! With Ben, I was in there the whole time. Ben got the healthiest in utero thing because I was in jail, couldn't do no drugs, I was going to the doctor. He got the number one best out of all of everything. I know he did because he was clean.

I really wanted to keep him, I really did. I really, really, really wanted to keep him. I'd figured out this was my new start. I was sober, I was getting away from Al—this baby will be clean. When I went into labor the social worker said I couldn't have him. I said, "Let me have my baby, it'll be sober because I've been in jail. I'll go to a drug program where I can have kids." She said, "Why don't you concentrate on getting Alex back." But I figured Alex was a lost cause because my dad had custody of him by this time.

My dad came up to the hospital and said, "Just let me talk to you. You can't keep the baby. You've got to go back to Alex and make it right, or try to make it right. You have to. I'll never forgive you if you don't. Because I've been hearing that child cry every night, crying for you, crying in the dentist chair because you neglected to take care of him. You haven't heard this child screaming in the night because he said someone's trying to get him. I've been there, and you haven't, and now you've gotta try to make it right."

He said, "Let this baby go. Maybe you're not supposed to be a mom. Maybe that time of your life is over, and you need to stop. Just please don't make a bigger mountain out of this than it is, don't add to it. You have to try to fix it, you have to go back to where you created the knot." I wish that I would have kept Ben, too. Not now, now that I think about it—that just would have made a bigger problem. Because now how old's Ben, four? I cannot deal with no frickin' four-year-old.

That day when I knew the adoptive parents were coming, oh my God, my heart, I just had to get out of there. The social worker came and said, "They're coming, so you might want to do your final . . ." And I didn't even say good-bye, because I said, "This isn't good-bye, not really." Because they're going to want to know who I am. If you've been adopted, you want to know, you can't help it, it's curiosity. But maybe they won't feel that way because Ben and his siblings are all three together. Maybe they won't be as interested in finding out because they have the comfort of each other. Whereas me being adopted and growing up, I felt estranged all the time. My dad said he never wanted me to know that I was adopted. I woulda rather had it that way. I wish they never would have told me. I never would have suspected.

When I was pregnant with Rachel, the one before Ben, I

came home, did a line, and that's what sent me into labor. With her and Hannah, the one before Rachel, I didn't feel labor pain because I was high. All I could do was get high. Rachel was really underweight. That's not good. Her lungs were so underdeveloped. The ambulance people came because they were transporting her to a hospital with neonatal. The paramedics came and they were putting her in the incubator, and I had to sign. The paramedic said, "I can't believe you did drugs when you were pregnant." I'll never forget the look on his face.

I put up five kids for adoption, and I'm ashamed. But I always felt like nobody could take that away from me. Nobody can take that from me. I made those kids. No matter how much the adoptive parents say, "These are my kids," they're not, they're mine. I made them, they came from me, they have my genes, they have my disposition. I know that they are good kids and all that, but it will come out later.

I feel like I did good with what I had to do, but that's kind of an excuse too, because we know I wanted money when I was pregnant. So I feel like I gave Rachel and Hannah up for adoption out of like survival almost, but I feel like I did right by them.

I used to be worried about all the kids coming to find me. Now I'm not—I kinda wish they would so they would know that I didn't do it out of spite or anything. "Come on down, calling everybody, come on down. See what you're glad you didn't get to witness. Come on down and be grateful." They ought to come and see what they got to miss. "We don't need to be buddies, because I might try to borrow money from you. So don't bug me, but come on down."

Looking at those photographs today of the three of them is like looking at a stranger's kids. It's almost like I was looking at them out of courtesy, but I wanted to see them. I don't know what I'm looking at. I never would have known that those were my kids. I don't even remember what they look like. I had a photograph of them but I don't have it anymore. If they were to come in to where I worked at and ate or something, I would never even know. They could have come up to me on the street and I probably would have said, "Hey, git!" I don't like kids. I don't like kids. They want too much attention, and then they bug you all the time, and then they get into your stuff, and leave you no time at all for yourself. I wanted something that nobody could take away, but they could have it. I'm just really selfish.

I do drugs because I think I am self-medicating. I don't think I have a mental disease, I think I have more like a chemical imbalance. They give you lithium, but it takes a couple months to get regulated on it. I like to smoke weed because it makes me feel like . . . you know when you were a little kid and you wore one of those little bumper things around you for the swimming pool? I feel like I got one of those on when I'm high. It doesn't matter what I bump into because it just bounces right off, it doesn't matter. You can say whatever you want to me, I don't care.

Speed makes me feel "I can do anything. I can fly, I can fly!" That's what gave me the strength to go into stores and steal right in their faces, and it didn't dawn on me I could get caught. I'd think about getting caught later. That's why I've got a chemical imbalance, that reasoning right there, that judgment of, "Now I know I shouldn't be doing this, and I know if I get caught I'm going to be fucked. Oh well, do it anyway— hope I don't get caught." Speed makes you feel like you're not going to get caught. That's why I'm doing it, because I don't want to think.

I'm strong personalitywise, but as far as anything else, Al has taken care of me my whole life. I don't even know what to do without Al. Someone has always told me what to do. Now Al won't have me. He's stable, he pays all his own bills, got credit cards, got a bank account, he's got car insurance. He takes care of Alex all by himself, and works a full-time job. He says, "This is how it would be if you came. We don't cuss, we don't do speed, we go to church on Sundays, and Alex goes to catechism on Wednesday night. My family can't stand you, Jane. How am I going to work you back in with my family?" He said, "I don't think you can do it, I don't think you're ready for it. I know you, Jane, and I don't think you could reform that much, and I don't want to set you up for failure. I don't want to tell you to come back and find out that you can't stop doing all the things that you do." He won't take me back.

He said, "You gotta have something that's your own individualized type life before you can come back to Alex and be successful. You'll never be successful unless you've got something of your own. If you had a job, and you had money, then you'd be able to contribute to the family unit. If I took you in now, all you would do is suck from the family unit, and I can't let you do that right now." I think it's true. See, I do good for a while, and then I screw up.

Last night I was with Al, and we were at the Laundromat. I was huggin' on Al, and Alex goes, "No, my dad, my dad." He said, "We don't need you. We've been doing just fine for two years without you." I said, "You better watch your mouth, because I'm not your dad and I'll backhand you one. You don't talk to me like that." Al said to Alex, "Go to the corner. Honor thy father and thy mother. You know what you've done. Go, git."

If Alex disrespects me, Al will discipline him and say, "You don't disrespect her. I don't care how much wrong she's done, I don't care if she's been around for two years or not, you don't disrespect her in front of me. You want to do that when I'm not around, you think you can get away with it, and I find out, I'm tappin' your rear end. Don't disrespect her ever."

And I told Al, "That makes me feel good." He said, "I ain't doing it for you, I'm doing it for him and God. Because the Bible tells me I gotta raise him to do right. And if I don't raise my son to do right, then I'm going to suffer. Whatever he does wrong, it's going to come back on me because I didn't teach him right. I ain't doing it for you, I ain't doing it for me, I'm doing it for God. Alex should be respectful to all adults, to anybody that's older than him and tells him what to do; he needs to have respect." Alex does mind Al.

Right now, I'm just waiting for him to ask me to come back. I don't feel right, I feel out of place, I feel like I need to be over there. I feel alive when I'm over there, I feel like

I'm interacting. I get tired of coming home every day and sitting on the bed.

I feel like if I don't go back, and I don't fix what I started, God's going to punish me. God's been talking to me lately, it's like, "Come on, you've had seven kids and you can't do right by one? Come on, you know, come on." That's what I feel, because when I was giving those babies up for adoption I would tell God, "Hey, I'm OK now because I did a good thing, right?" And He would tell me, "You didn't do good— baby's on drugs. You didn't do no good. Don't be asking about points because you're not getting none."

Everyone makes mistakes. If you have a baby, just because you make one doesn't mean you're able to take care of it. Maybe God had me get pregnant all those times for the adoptive parents. Maybe that was meant to be. They say God uses people as vessels; maybe that's what I'm here to do. Maybe I've done my thing. And maybe it bothers me, but maybe God knew that I could do that—I could have a baby and give it up. I can.

Everyone should think, Don't have kids! There should be a regulation, because some people aren't cut out for it. But I do believe when Judgment Day comes God's going to say, "I know what bad you've done. What good have you done?" You know damn well what I'm going to say, I'm going to say the names of all my kids. I tried to do right, and that's why I feel like I gotta go back with Alex.

Update

JANE RECENTLY COMPLETED a course to become a medical assistant. Her goal is to find a job, and to rebuild her relationship with her son Alex.

Comments

JANE PLACED THREE of her children—Ben, Rachel, and Hannah—with my clients, a fact she never makes completely clear. In our five-hour interview I had a very hard time getting her to focus on the adoption stories; she wanted to talk about everything else but those kids.

She is the birthmother everyone fears, the only birthmother I have ever known who admitted she planned to deceive adoptive parents because she needed money. I hesitated to include Jane's story in this collection because her life has been filled with so many awful experiences, from the neglect she endured as an infant, to her downhill slide into drugs, to the birth of seven children in seven years, none of whom she managed to keep. I feared that her story was so sad, so raunchy, that she would receive only condemnation, and miss out on the compassion generally felt for birthmothers.

I decided to keep her interview in the book to illustrate one of the most important aspects of adoption: future contact. Jane is unlike most birthmothers in that she did not reserve the right to receive photographs of her children in the years after their birth. But she has something in common with almost all the birthmothers I have ever known: She feels guilt and shame because she placed her children for adoption. One might think pride or satisfaction would predominate, but at least for a period of time, it is guilt that haunts them. Birthmothers choose independent adoption because it allows them to decide upon the adoptive family, and to receive photographs each year. These two things help to transform the guilt into confidence that a good choice has been made. The yearly photographs in particular give birthmothers comfort, and are of great importance to them.

What happens when the adoptive parents stop sending photographs, or when, in the unusual case of promised visitation, the adoptive parents tell the birthmother she is no longer welcome in their lives? Nothing. There is no legislation in most states that would make even written promises enforceable in nonrelative adoptions. Only in 2002 did California develop postadoption contact agreements that are filed with the court before an adoption is final. They allow a birthmother to take the adoptive parents back into court if they fail to keep their future contact promises to her. How effective they will be is uncertain, because the agreements are clear that the validity of the adoption may not be challenged. What sanctions are available is not mentioned.

Most adoptive parents are kind and honorable and would not discontinue sending photos, even though as the years go by many become annoyed by it and ask, "Isn't it time she moved on? Do I still have to send these?" For they realize the magnitude of the gift given to them by the birthmother and keep their word, even when it is inconvenient, or they would rather stop. They also understand that once the child is grown and searches out his or her birthparents, the truth about any broken promises will be known, and it is to their advantage to uphold the agreement.

The status of the law encourages adoptive parents to believe that they are within their rights to do anything they want with respect to a birthmother after finalization of the adoption, and places them in a difficult moral position. When a birthmother and adoptive parents first meet and are discussing their desires, it is tempting for the adoptive parents to agree to whatever the birthmother requests. Once the child is a few years old those promises may be forgotten or ignored with impunity.

Adoptive parents have the security of knowing that once the adoption is final, assuming all procedures were done correctly, and absent fraud or duress, nothing can threaten their newly formed family. Birthmothers have no certainty they will ever receive another picture of their child, see them again, be assured of their well-being, or even know in what state or country they are being raised.

As small a matter as yearly photographs or visitation might seem to some, to a birthmother who places her child for adoption with that as part of the arrangement, they are of the utmost importance. Even Jane regrets the fact that she doesn't receive photographs. Because of her continued drug use, and her and the birthfather's return trips to jail, the adoptive parents are not comfortable agreeing to that now. They send photographs to me and have given me permission to show them to her. Before our meeting Jane reminded me repeatedly to be sure and bring the photographs of her children. When

I arrived she glanced at one or two of them, but quickly put them aside and never finished looking at them. It was hard to tell if her seeming disinterest in them was real, or a mask for other emotions.

There needs to be a meaningful, balanced law that serves equally the rights and needs of the birthmother and the adoptive parents. A discretionary promise that can be withdrawn at will, without consequences, is not worthy of adoption, not respectful of the profound act of giving one's child to another.

9

A New American Family

GLORIA

An adoptive mother

*"In my life I have suffered a lot. Now, after all of this—
the alleged kidnapping, the adoptions—I have a whole
new life, a beautiful life."*

I was born in Ecuador. I think of my grandmother as my real mother because she had such a big part in my upbringing. When I was four or five years old my mother remarried; I hated my stepfather. I would make up lies and tell my grandmother, "Grandma, he tried to bite me!" or, "Grandma, he takes food away from me to give to his own children!" One time he said to me, "You're a queer." This time he was right.

He could tell I was different because I would play with my sister's dolls and toys, and dance around for everyone. I would look at my sister and say, I want to dress that way, too. I didn't say that out loud, only to myself, because I would have been killed in Ecuador for saying such a thing. They would take me to the river and throw me in, saying, "That's the end of your life. Go!" In my country it's impossible to be a homosexual, it's a crime. My stepfather and my sister were the only ones who knew my secret. My sister would say to me, "Oh, you're just like a little girl," and I would feel embarrassed.

When I was nine years old my stepfather moved from the country to the city to find work, and my mother and I went with him. I loved the idea. Ah, the city, I'd think, They have lights and nice houses. We were desperately poor, in part because my mother made the mistake of marrying my stepfather. Everything that she owned—the land, everything—he sold.

I found a job as a helper in the house of some rich people. I would help bring things back from the market, I cleaned windows, anything that needed to be done. I made a hundred sucres every thirty days, which is about one dollar. After I worked with them for six months, my family moved back to the country. A year later I ran away. I said to myself, I'm not going to stay in this kind of life. I know the city, and I'm going to get back there. So I ran away.

Not too long after a friend of mine said, "How would you like a job learning how to sew and make clothes?" I said yes. I learned to make pants, shirts, and I was making good money, about $12 a day. That money went straight to my mom and her kids. Then I found a job in another city at a gas station, putting gas in people's cars; it paid 400 sucres a month. I gave 200 to my mom and I kept 200 to pay for school. This was when I was beginning high school, eighth, ninth, tenth, and starting in the eleventh grade.

Around that time one of my cousins went to the United States, and then another followed. But those cousins and everybody else said, "Well, Jorge is a weird kind of kid. He's obviously lazy, because he likes women's work. He's not going to make it in the United States." Everyone suspected by that time who I was, that I was gay, or queer, and they thought I would be embarrassing them in the United States, or anywhere that I went. But one cousin said, "OK, I'm going to send you nine hundred dollars, and with that money get your visa, get your money in the bank, and do everything else you need to do so that you can come to the United States, and we'll get together then." That's what I did, and I came to Newark, New Jersey.

When I arrived in the United States I said to myself, Wow, it's just like my grandmother told me it would be—it's heaven. This is the kind of life I want. I saw a sign in the Puerto Rican community that said, "Opportunity! Learn English and Get a Job!" They spoke Spanish there, and I said, "I need a job and I need to go to school." They said, "Welcome. This is the place for you." They told me, "We pay you two dollars and five cents per hour. You can work ten hours, and go as many hours as you want to learn English." That's where I learned to speak English, and I made $134 a week at my job.

Then I found a second job at a Catholic college working Saturdays and Sundays. I washed my own clothes, I made my own food. I did everything so that the most I spent each week was $15 on rent and food. In nine months I finished high school.

At that time there was an earthquake in Ecuador, and a lot of the country was destroyed. My teacher spoke to me and she said, "Are you OK? Because you look so sad, and I know what happened with the earthquake in Ecuador." She collected money from all the students and teachers and gave me $200. I said, "What is this for?" "This is for you to send to your mom back home." And I said to myself, This country is something else, these people really have a heart. These people are totally different from the people in my country.

When I finished high school a teacher, a Cuban lady, said to me, "Now it's time for you to go to college." I said, "How?" She said, "We'll get you a student visa." And she and some people from Rutgers University helped me with that. When Newark International Airport opened there were a lot of job opportunities. I filled out an application and in three weeks they called me and said, "OK, go to Miami for your training." I was very, very nervous, but I learned computers and everything. I was bilingual by that time, and a friend of mine said, "Let's go apply for Pan Am," because Pan Am was an international airline. I was hired by Pan Am and in the application it asked, "Would you like to be relocated?" I answered, "Yes." So, after six months I was relocated, and that's when I went to Israel, Paris, Frankfurt, Japan. When I was stationed in Paris I used to go to a lot of countries. I went to Saudi Arabia, I went to Baghdad, Jordan, Egypt. I used to travel every fifteen days with different people.

I felt very free then; everything that I'd ever dreamed of

was coming true. But I still had the responsibility of my mom and my brothers and sisters. I was making $16,200 a year, which back then was a huge amount of money. I started building a $40,000 house for my mom. Then I bought her a farm in Ecuador, a brand-new truck, I hired housekeepers for her. But she never appreciated what I did. She thought everything in the United States is free, which of course is not true.

Also, I was always thinking in the back of my mind, I wish I could be a woman. But I wasn't. I was dressing like a man in uniforms and suits and everything, and living like one. I suspected that by then a lot of people knew I was homosexual. I was living one life, but inside I was living another very different life. I wasn't a man—my feelings were the feelings of a woman. I would ask myself, When am I going to be a woman—when, how? I had a friend Ruben who worked at TWA. He liked me and sometimes we'd go to parties together, not as dates but as friends. One day he said, "Jorge, I understand who you are inside and I want to help you." And this was a straight man, he said, "I'm going to help you. I know your family, and I understand how much you are suffering right now because inside you are something different. You're still pretending you're a man, but you are not a man."

He was the one who really made me understand that I could be a woman. He said, "Let's go to Bellevue Hospital in New York—they are the hospital that does this kind of surgery." The doctor we spoke to there said, "Yes, we can perform this kind of surgery, but it is still a rare procedure." He said, "Do you understand how much this is going to cost? The surgery itself is twenty-two thousand dollars, but with everything the average cost is a hundred twenty thousand." But from then on, I was clear in my mind that, yes, I can do this, if I start saving my money I can make it.

I made a very clear decision then to start my new life in California, just like I once left Ecuador and started my new life in the United States. Shortly after I moved to California I was in my car, drinking a beer. It's embarrassing to talk about this, but I need to tell the truth about things. A policeman saw me and stopped me. I said, "Yes, I am drinking a beer. Is that illegal?" I asked because in New Jersey it was still legal to drink in the car. It turns out it was illegal. I pleaded guilty and had to pay a $32 fine; I went to jail for a little while too. It was in the jail that I met Luis, Roberto's father. He was a very, very nice person, a beautiful person. Of course, I was scared, I'd never been in jail before. When we got out he gave me his number; even without a pen I remembered it.

He was a good friend, and he could see who I really was. He said, "You are like an orphan—you don't have a family, you don't have anybody. You are a nobody, just like me." He was very protective of me. If I was going on a date with someone he would say, "OK, if you are meeting someone new, don't wear your jewelry. Don't let them pick you up—I will drive you to meet them." He really helped me out in a lot of ways, even though later it turned out to be very bad.

One day I saw my husband, Diego, for the very first time. I had just gotten out of work, and I was in my uniform. He saw me, and I was looking back at him, and I said to myself, What a handsome guy, nice-looking man. Because I had been alone for too many years. He said, "So, do you work for immigration or something?" Because he could see my Pan Am tag. I said, "No, I work for the airline." He said, "Where are you going?" I said, "I'm going home." I asked him, "Where are you going?" He said, "I don't know. I don't have anyplace to go." So I said, "Let's go have a drink." He said, "No, I don't drink," but that turned out to be a lie!

But even from that very first day I could tell he was a very, very nice person. He told me his life story, all about his mom and dad, and how he used to sleep in Dumpsters. He had basically been a homeless kid, and he had been very young at the time. He was already going back and forth between Los Angeles and Mexico by the time he was thirteen years old. At that time Diego was into many bad things—I mean, he was a street kid. But after about a week he said, "Hey, I need you and you need me. Let's get together." After one month I knew I couldn't live without him. I knew that this was the man that I needed.

Shortly after that I said, "We need to buy a house." He said, "How are we going to get money for that?" I said, "I have the money," because I had $27,000 in my savings. So after two months of knowing each other we bought a house. Then we brought Diego's baby up from Mexico; he was just eight months old. This was a child Diego had with an old girlfriend. And pretty soon his nine-year-old brother joined us, and we began to raise him too.

I helped Diego get started in landscaping. I bought him a truck, and I helped him find a lot of work. He was making about $2,000 a week. He was so happy; his baby was here, and his little brother. He had everything he needed to make him happy. And that was the beginning of my real life too. I had my husband, I had my children. I called him my husband, but only at home in our hidden life. We could never openly show that part of our lives in public.

One day I told him, "I have a friend Ruben who told me that with surgery I could become a woman." Diego said, "OK, if you are going to be a woman, you can be my woman. But if you don't, we can't be together forever, because I need a woman." He said, "I am a man, and I'm OK with you as a man and the way we are, but not for the rest of my life."

After psychological testing that determined I was ready for the operation, I began the treatment. A combination of surgeries and hormone treatments—which took years—made me into a woman. [Jorge then legally changed his name to Gloria.]

Although my husband and I had been together for a long time, we were able to get married legally after that. During that time we were raising Roberto, Luis's son, the man I met in jail. It was like having an entirely new life for me. Here I was a woman, I was married, Roberto was a lovely boy, and we both loved him very much. He lived with us for six years; in fact, he was born in our home. But one day Luis accused us of kidnapping Roberto and everything good seemed to drop out of my life. We had everything we could ever want—beautiful homes, cars, money, business—but one of our sons was gone.

I was accused of kidnapping because Roberto went with me wherever I would go, to California, Houston, Ecuador, New York, Hawaii, Europe—anywhere that I went, he went with me. Diego and I had power of attorney regarding Roberto, but not adoption papers. These rights were given to me in writing by Luis and by his wife through an attorney. I had the right to make decisions about his education, to travel with him, and all the other things a parent can do. Luis denied that he signed the papers, claiming I had falsified them because I knew how to use computers. That was the big accusation.

I knew Luis wasn't the one behind all this—it was his wife. His wife wanted the child back because she was so jealous that Roberto was with me. Roberto didn't like her. One time he told her, "Hey, you're not my mom." That's when she got mad and said, "OK, this boy is coming back to me."

I fought until the end. They offered us so many chances to compromise; they'd say, "Here's our offer—three years in jail and five probation." I said, "No, not one day." Then they said, "OK, one year in jail and two years probation." I said, "No." Then they said, "Three months in jail, one year probation." I said, "No."

Three times we went to court. One time the judge said, "Gloria, if you want to plead guilty, this is your opportunity. You could accept the offer of three months now, or risk fifteen years in jail if the jury finds you guilty." I said, "No, I want to take this to the end. If I made a mistake in my life, then let me pay for it. But in this case I didn't make any mistakes, I am telling the truth, and let's go for the truth." The judge said, "OK, very good."

One day I was in the cafeteria waiting for the start of the trial. I was so nervous I couldn't even drink coffee. The prosecutor went to speak with my attorney and then my attorney said to me, "Gloria, here's what's happening: The case is over." I said,

"What do you mean it's over? There's not going to be a trial?" He said, "No, he doesn't have a case." I said, "What do you mean 'he doesn't have a case'?" I mean, the prosecutor didn't have a case! He had been lying to my attorney saying he had witnesses and all sorts of evidence, but he didn't have anything.

My psychologist was willing to testify for us, and two of my main doctors were going to be witnesses. I had letters and all sorts of things that supported us. The worst one for them was from the psychologist. She wrote a letter to the court explaining just what kind of damage they were doing to me and Diego, and how it was really affecting Diego so that he was beginning to think he was married to a man instead of a woman. Because they would only call me Jorge. The psychologist said, "Please stop this; don't call her Jorge anymore." I was a woman, and they knew it. I had records from the hospital, from the court when I assumed my new name, everything was ready and in order, but they still insisted, "Look, you're Jorge." The psychologist explained to them that there is federal law that states that when a gender change is done and legal, it's a crime to be treating the person as if none of it had happened.

What was really happening is that people think that homosexuals or gay people are desperate to have kids, and that they don't have access to adopt children. So the case was based upon this idea that me and Diego, two guys, stole the baby because we couldn't get one any other way. That's where the kidnapping charge came in. The law left us completely unprotected from this kind of charge.

When we won Diego's attorney said, "All right, now that we've won, we are going to countersue and ask a million dollars in damages for Diego and a million dollars for Gloria for the destruction they've done to your lives, and to get back all the money you've spent fighting this." They were already preparing all the papers. If we had gone for a trial I think Luis would be in jail for all his lies. They asked me, "How much do you want from this guy?" I said, "If I won the case, then just let it go." I told the attorney, "I can forgive my enemies; I don't want enemies. I want to be at peace with people through the way I'm living in the world." I tried to show him that I'm not vindictive. I mean, there have been enough problems in my life. But I don't hate anybody, and I don't indulge in revenge. I accept what happens—that's life. [The kidnapping charges were dropped, but Roberto went to live with Luis, and Gloria and Diego were forbidden to see him.]

By now my two other kids, Diego's son and brother, were getting big, but there were so many reminders of Roberto around. That's why we sold the house, because there was the swimming pool where he played all the time, and little things he'd left around the house, toys we'd find outside. One time at sunset I saw Diego outside crying, it was almost dark. I said, "What's wrong?" He said, "I just found something that Roberto left." So I said to one of my sons, "Let's sell this house and find another house without all these memories." But I saved all his toys.

That's when I decided I was going to pursue adoption; I decided I was going to adopt maybe two kids. The attorney I used to defend me in the kidnapping case said, "You have the right to adopt; you can do whatever you want. Your life and your name are now free and clear. You can do what you want to do." All the fear and threat of the kidnapping trial was gone, and my lawyer told me I was free to resume my life.

I consulted with a doctor I trust and he said, "Gloria, you are a mom. You've already raised two kids, and you can raise as many as you want. No one can stop you from this now. You are a woman, and your life is getting back to normal. Just say, 'I am Gloria, I am married, I have a husband, and I am a woman. I can adopt children if I want to.'"

My attorney told me that the best way to go about it was to use a private agency. I asked him where to find one and he said, "Just look in the yellow pages." I did, and I found a facilitator. I called them and they said, "Sure, come on over." We went there and I acted just like any other married woman, but my husband and I never revealed to them anything about my life before I was Gloria. After we left I said, "Wait a minute, we're lying about this even if we didn't say anything."

I went back and we told them everything. They said, "Don't worry, that's fine." That was in January. In April they called me and said, "We have a baby for you." Two or three people had already turned down this birthmother because she was homeless or because she was Korean. I said, "I don't care what she is. I want this baby."

I went to see her in the homeless hotel. The first thing that I felt was, This poor woman. She was living like an animal. She had not much more than soup in a cup to eat that she made in her room. I said to myself, This is the woman I want.

I don't need someone with a beautiful face or a more stable life, because they don't need me. She is going to be delivering a beautiful child, as beautiful as any flower.

I asked her if she would have us as the adoptive parents of her child, and she said, "Yes, this is going to be your baby." We took care of her physical and medical needs from that time until she delivered the baby. First you told her, but then I wanted to tell her again myself. I said, "Here is my situation: I am a transsexual." She said, "Are you a woman now?" I said, "Yes, I am." She asked, "Are you married?" "Yes." She said, "Then I don't care, I don't care." She asked me very few questions about it. She said, "That's OK with me," and that was about it. When my son was born he was a beautiful baby, and it made me feel alive again, like my life was beginning again. I felt like a mother from the first day that I had him.

Everything went smoothly until the day we went to court to finalize the adoption. In court we saw the same judge who presided at part of the kidnapping trial. He looked at us and said, "Wait a minute, this could be complicated." He remembered the past, but he didn't know how everything had turned out, so he thought we were trying to pull a fast one or something. We had to come back but when we showed him all the papers clearing our name he finally said, "OK, everything is settled, everything is fine." I think he really understood that all the accusations against me and Diego were false. I think he realized I wasn't some kind of pervert, that I lived a good life and lived in a nice area. I mean, he had my entire life there in front of him in the paperwork—my taxes, my business—he knew everything there was to know about me. He changed his mind about us, but I think in the beginning he was a little prejudiced against us. Then we had the hearing and he said those wonderful words: "This child is now your son, Diego, Jr."

Not too long after that we decided to search for another child, and we found our daughter Angelina. I wanted another boy and Diego wanted a girl, so we just decided to go ahead and whatever it was would be fine with us. We met our daughter's birthmother, Carmen. She was just a little teeny thing, a beautiful Hispanic girl. She hinted that there had been some big problems in her life [a former gang affiliation]. But I thought, Her problems are not going to go with her baby. The baby is going to be raised by us without the influences of her life; that's separate. I said to Diego, "This is a nice girl, a decent girl." He said, "OK, let's see if we can adopt her baby."

So with Carmen I had to go through the same explanation that I went through with our first birthmother. She asked me, "Are you legally a woman and everything?" I said, "Yes." She said, "I don't really care. If you're a woman now; I don't care about what came before." She didn't really let me explain much or want me to go into too much detail. And it was that open-mindedness that helped me accept her for what she was, too. It didn't matter to me what she had done in the past.

We did have a big problem, though, after we'd had the baby almost three months, the exact amount of time Carmen had to change her mind. She called me and said she wanted the baby back. I said, "OK, but talk to our attorney." We made

arrangements to have a meeting with the lawyer and the social worker who had helped us, and we all met.

It turns out what she really wanted was just to see the baby
during the next two or three years. I was totally OK with that,
and I was so glad that was her only problem with the adoption. We're like old friends now; we talk on the phone, and
we got together with her one time already to show her Angelina. She didn't even touch her. She just said, "Your baby's
so beautiful." Then in December I sent her pictures and a
little gift. She called and said, "Gloria, how beautiful your
daughter is."

So, that's just about where our lives are now. I think that
will be our last adoption. Soon I'll be ready to travel anywhere
I want, which is my real dream—to travel with my family.
We've been lots of places in the United States together, but
not outside. I am not going to leave any money in my bank
accounts when I die because that will only cause problems. I
want to provide good lives, and lots of culture for my children
now, and nice houses to live in. But I want to spend all my
money on trips and show them what life is about, and show
them other countries.

It's hard for me to offer suggestions about how adoption
law could be changed, because it seems so rigid the way it is
now. It is going to take a lot of people getting together and
asking, "What are you doing to these poor kids, ruining these
innocent lives?" And if the baby is placed by an agency or the
government or whoever for adoption, that should be final. It
should be, "OK, this is your baby without restrictions." There
should not be a three-month waiting period that says, "Well,

if she changes her mind the baby's going to be gone." The hardest part of raising a child is those first three months; you are dedicating all your time to the baby. And the nighttime is really hard! With my children I stayed right next to them for the first fifteen days, cuddling them in bed. I'd go from the kitchen to the bed; I felt like a mother bird feeding them their little bottles and keeping them alive. That's what you have to do with babies.

Now, anywhere that I go, any trip that I take, my kids go with me. My kids are never watched by strangers or sitters. They are secure, knowing they have food, warmth, Mommy and Daddy, they have a safe yard to run in, they have everything.

In my life I have suffered a lot. Now, after all of this—the alleged kidnapping, the adoptions—I have a whole new life, a beautiful life. I am truly a woman; I can dress as a woman, I can face anyone proudly. Let me put it this way: If I was stopped by the police and they ran my records and said, "Who is Jorge?" I would say, "I don't know. Who is Jorge?" Because I know with certainty I am no longer Jorge.

Update

GLORIA CONTINUES TO conquer the business world, while happily raising her two small children with Diego. In the fall of 2000 she sent one of her older sons off to college, while the other one continues to advise and assist her in some of her more lucrative ventures.

Comment

I FIRST MET Gloria when she came to my office to discuss the details of her proposed adoption. At that time I had no idea what Gloria's "secret" was, but I could tell there was something on her mind that she was about to divulge, however reluctantly. I anticipated a commonplace problem such as a minor criminal offense or unsettled immigration status.

When she told me she had not always been a woman, I was able to accept it and her immediately. She had a deep spiritual quality often seen in people who have experienced a lot of suffering. It drew me in and made me want to help her and to be protective of her. Gloria takes great care with her appearance, dressing in well-tailored suits with tasteful accessories. I have been told since I met her that a man's hands or calf muscles will betray him even after his surgeries and hormone treatments, but that is not true of Gloria. She looks like what she is—an intelligent, aware, and successful woman.

I explained that we would have to disclose the fact that she was a transsexual to the birthmother who had just chosen to work with her and Diego; she looked doubtful and troubled, not at all sure a birthmother would accept her once she knew. I made no guarantees about the attitudes of Children's Services, which would be doing their home study, or of the court, but promised to begin my investigations immediately. This was completely new territory for me and I could only share my hope that the necessary approvals would be given.

The birthmother who had chosen Gloria and Diego lived in a hotel for the homeless with her three-year-old daughter.

I am used to going to dangerous neighborhoods to meet birth-mothers, but even I was afraid to go down the long, dark hall of the run-down hotel to the birthmother's room, unsure of what unpleasantness or violence might await me. I insisted to the annoyed desk clerk that she must go and get the birth-mother and bring her to the lobby. The birthmother had been a middle-class wife and mother until her husband had tired of her and threw her out of their home so that his girlfriend could move in. Her first language was not English, although she had been speaking it for years. Because of this I was par-ticularly careful and simple in the way I explained Gloria's situation to her. She nodded her head thoughtfully and finally said, "I don't care. That doesn't matter to me." I offered to explain or clarify any aspect of Gloria and Diego's life she wanted to know about, but she was not interested in more details. She had talked and met with Gloria and liked her and her family, and that was what mattered to her. Our first legal hurdle had now been cleared; the birthmother knew the facts and wanted to proceed.

Shortly after receiving the birthmother's approval of Gloria and Diego, I contacted Children's Services and asked the di-rector if they would have a problem with an adoption by a married transsexual. She was taken aback and said that al-though they had never encountered the situation before, they would give it a fair hearing. She kept her word, but there were extra requirements demanded for the adoption, mostly documentation from psychologists about the mental and emo-tional stability of the couple.

During the rest of the pregnancy and even after the birth,

I watched Gloria set the standard for a dedicated and caring adoptive parent. Within a week of meeting the birthmother she had found an apartment for her and filled it with all the little comforts she knew the birthmother would appreciate. If her birthmother needed food money and waited until the last minute to ask for it, Gloria would drive the three-hour round trip to her apartment and make sure she had everything she needed. Gloria's own early poverty and suffering made her a particularly kind and generous adoptive mother.

The birth went well, and when I went to the hospital to visit the birthmother she talked to me for a long time about her life. Her father was a published poet of whom she was very proud. Her husband, who was not the father of this baby, worked for a powerful government agency, and regularly beat and humiliated her. She expressed her relief that this baby would be safe and happy with Gloria and Diego, and longed for the same thing for her daughter. Her soon-to-be ex-husband, whom I spoke to only once, was extremely unpleasant during our conversation, insisting on knowing "how much she sold the baby for," alternately threatening to call the police and demanding a portion of the imaginary proceeds.

The home study began and the social worker who was assigned to Gloria's case fell under her spell, just as I had, and they became great friends. When the time came she wrote a report to the court recommending the adoption and assuring the court the child would have an excellent family and home life.

The morning that Gloria, Diego, their baby, their two older sons and I filed into court for our final hearing, I could tell immediately from the judge's face that all was not well. He recognized Gloria and Diego from their appearances before him for the California part of the kidnapping trial. Although everything was supposed to have been reviewed and approved before the hearing, to our surprise and disappointment he chose not to finalize the adoption that day. He wanted to satisfy himself through written proof that the kidnapping issues had been resolved in Gloria and Diego's favor, and that it was in the child's best interest to be adopted by them.

He assigned the child a court-appointed lawyer, and after a few months it was clear to the court that much injustice had been done to Gloria and Diego with the kidnapping trial. Aside from the glowing reports from the psychologists who had known them for years, the fact that Gloria still maintained a six-figure trust account for Roberto, whom she and Diego had been accused of kidnapping, impressed the court-appointed lawyer. He saw her true love for the boy and her lack of vindictiveness toward the child's biological parents, who although they had threatened every aspect of her life were still employed at one of Gloria's restaurants.

In another state, in another county even, or with another judge, this family could easily have been denied the right to adopt their son. Our Los Angeles County adoption judge is an experienced jurist and a fair-minded man. Whatever skepticism he had was overcome by the facts, and he did not allow prejudice to cloud his judgment. I have seen judges in other counties act with rudeness and hostility toward gay adoptive parents, spending the least amount of time possible to finalize their adoptions and get them out of their courtrooms, not bothering to conceal their distaste and anger. How much angrier would they have been with the even more unusual case of a transsexual adoptive mother, and how much more leeway would they have had to deny the adoption? The fact that the system can be so arbitrary makes it very difficult to advise clients like Gloria on what the outcome of their adoption might be.

There are no laws I am aware of that speak to adoption by transsexuals. Gloria's status as a transgender woman is not covered by laws and policies governing gay adoption, because she is a legally married woman and a heterosexual. Problems for transgender adoptive parents are as likely to stem from fear and ignorance as from the law. They will be at the mercy of the investigating social worker and the attitudes of the court, as well as of the laws of the state where they live. I was unable to find statistics on transgender adoption, but it is unlikely that a state that forbids or discourages adoption by homosexuals would welcome adoption by a transgender man or woman. A recent Vatican newsletter called a decision by a Spanish court to allow a transsexual to adopt "repugnant" and an insult to the institution of the family. Acceptance is not going to come fast or easily.

Gloria's strength and goodness shine so bright that everyone who met her in the adoption process liked and accepted her, and after the long and difficult first adoption, the second one went smoothly, as did the adoption of her two older boys. But the depth of the scorn aimed at her by the FBI during the kidnapping incident revealed what type of treatment she could have expected as an adoptive parent in some jurisdictions. The prosecutor insisted on calling her Jorge even though she was legally a woman, and was willing to send her to prison for fifteen years while knowing that the facts did not support his case.

For all the problems Gloria endured, a different type of prejudice worked in her favor: Her success and wealth helped her greatly in her adoption. It isn't that she used them to indulge a birthmother or influence the court, but rather that they lent her credibility in people's eyes. I saw the pattern again and again. There'd be the initial shock of hearing of her sex change, and then someone would comment on how prosperous she looked, or how well dressed. The fact that she was a transsexual, something few people can relate to personally, became secondary to her success, and her power in the business world. I believe the hard truth is that if Gloria had been a restaurant worker rather than the owner of a chain of restaurants, things might have gone differently for her, especially with the FBI.

Gloria took me completely by surprise when she told me she did not think lesbians and gays should be allowed to adopt because children need to have a mom and a dad. In the weeks after our interview she referred to this comment several times, knowing how unlikely this attitude was coming from her. All my arguments to the contrary fell on deaf ears, which should not have surprised me, considering that Gloria has spent her life trying to become a woman and part of a straight couple. She might be the least likely person to endorse gay adoption! She did finally say, "Well, really, the law is written on the heart and not on the paper." But, especially for adoption by nontraditional families, we need to make sure that pen, paper, and legislation are all involved.

In independent adoption, adoptive families are investigated in the months *after* the child is in their home. It is a great trauma and injustice to deny an adoption at that time—after the birthmother thinks she's found a secure home for her child, after the child has bonded to the adoptive parents, and after the adoptive parents think they are a family and the permanent parents of the child. This problem could be eliminated simply by requiring that home studies be done before a child may come into the home. Adoptive families need to know exactly what the laws are, and they must know in advance what their chances of a successful adoption are. The lawmakers and social services must give us clear, uniform laws and guidelines, not ones that are affected by the county a family lives in or the judge they are assigned. They affect every adoptive parent, not just nontraditional ones like Gloria and Diego.

10

Never Too Old

MICKEY

An adoptive father

"I didn't want to shrivel up to be a bitter old man. I still have a need to love, and to be loved in return."

I've been in California since I was ten years old, and that's approximately forty-seven years. I was born in Buffalo. A cousin of mine came here when she was about eighteen, and just talked about Venice Beach as if it was Shangri-la. We'd see pictures of how beautiful this place was while we were in six feet of snow and maybe 40 below zero. It had the ocean, the palm trees, a feeling of tranquillity, small homes, people that went about their business—there was a good feeling to it. Wherever I've been, to me this is always home. It always will be. I need a place that has roots, and my roots are here.

I work for the City of Los Angeles at the Venice Beach Boardwalk. The Boardwalk is a combination of retail shops and two miles where you can walk where car traffic is not permitted, right next to the sand and the Pacific Ocean. To my mind it's the Champs Élysées of the western part of the United States. This will be my twenty-third year of service for the city.

I'm single, and divorced, and I have one son who is thirty-three. We've had no contact whatsoever for four years. It was his decision not to see me. Why specifically, I do not know. He's a professor, and seeing that in layman's terms I'm an elite garbageman, I think he kind of resents that.

My earliest memory of my first adopted son Sean was a blond kid with lots of acne on his face, and a school bag. He was out there a lot, out on the Boardwalk and the beach, and I thought, I wonder does he have a home, or does he belong to someone—that was my first curiosity. He was with other kids his age, which must have been at that time thirteen or fourteen. I kind of made it my business to talk to him; he struck a chord in me, I don't know why. I felt sorry for him, I guess. I'd say, "Hello, how are you doing?" Or, "Where's your friends today, can I get you a soda," that type of thing. Of course, a kid is going to be wary of a man twenty-something years older than him. I understood that. Then one day he said to me, "What are you doing later? I'm kind of hungry." I said, "Well, OK," and I took him to dinner.

As time went by I would see him quite often and he would say to me, "Tell everybody that we meet that I'm your kid"— that's how he put it. So I did. And when people that I work with would ask me I would refer to him as my son. I found out he was adopted at birth. His adoptive parents thought they could have none of their own, but eventually they had some of their own, as far as I recall the story.

He had told me that he was in an accident at eleven years old. He had a skateboard and he rode it down the driveway and was battered down by a car. He was hurt very badly—they had to do a tracheotomy. He couldn't walk for about a year, and he was not expected to live at one point. Psychologically he seemed to be disoriented after that. He got involved in maybe drugs or alcohol. He became a pain and his adoptive parents wanted to give him back to the adoption agency. They tried to, but he ran away and that's how I met him.

I've never met them; I only know what he's told me. But I have to say to myself, They couldn't be the best, otherwise he'd still be with them. So there must have been some kind of a dysfunctional relationship there. I'm sure they have their side of the story also, but how conscionable can it be where somebody throws a thirteen- or fourteen-year-old out in the street or sends them back for adoption?

He was hell-bent against any authority, particularly the police department. He didn't want to live by the same rules as the rest of us. He seemed to have a fondness for some of the dredges of humanity; that's where he felt comfortable. He stayed with some of these people until Divine Providence provided him with me.

When Sean misbehaved I'd always know about it and tell him. He was amazed how I knew. I said to him, "Well, you've heard of the CIA, haven't you?" He said, "Yes." I said, "But I bet you haven't heard of the MIA—'Mickey's Intelligence

Agency.' I can find out anything that I want to, so you can't hide anything." Being in city work for most of my life, I'm blessed with a few people who give me information, and it's come in handy many, many times.

There were times he stayed away from me for a while, and then he'd call me back. It's like somebody getting used to you and kind of running away, and getting used to you again, which I could understand. You're developing a relationship. But under these circumstances it's amazing it did become what it did. It was like a seed that was planted, but it was not assured that it would ever reach full bloom. I think on one hand me being a minor city official made him feel good that, you know, here was a man in uniform that he could say, even before he was adopted, "This is my dad." I gave him a kind of, for lack of a better word, a certain legitimacy.

I included him in family functions; I encouraged him to get some schooling. If I was going to be interviewed on TV about something about the Boardwalk, I called him out. I wanted him to actually see it so he could be part of it. His story and mine got around, and of course, to the skeptics I was naive; to the other ones I was creating a situation for probably what they would think was some kind of undercover type of sexual relationship. Very few people really gave me the credence that here I was a middle-aged man trying to do something for a teenage boy. I didn't do it to make myself look good; I didn't have an ulterior motive. But some power somewhere made it happen. He needed a dad, I needed a kid.

And some of the things I suffered through. I mean, there were times he was in jail, I'd get a call, the operator would be on saying I got a call from Theo Lacey. And dumb as I am I said, "I don't know a Theo Lacey." "Well, sir, Theo Lacey is the men's jail." And I'd say, "Well, I know it couldn't be for me. Who would I know in the men's jail?" And it turned out to be him.

I looked in the mirror, and I said, I must be the biggest fool that ever lived. I got myself a pack of trouble now. Because at first I did say to myself, What a good man I am. I'm a wonderful human being—look what I did. Then suddenly, here came the jail thing, here came drug-related problems, all kinds of things. So here's your challenge—are you a real dad? Well, I was. I went to jail, I went to visit him.

I risked our relationship many times by telling him what I did not like—for instance, selling drugs. I'm not a puritan, I'm not a saint. But I've learned that doing the law-abiding thing is the right way to go; telling the truth. I told him how I felt, and sometimes very bluntly, sometimes fifty decibels above normal, right in the middle of the street, bringing traffic to a stop in four directions. He would tell me, "You don't really love me. You're just a bitter old man." Oh yes, that happened many times. But I had to risk his rejection to maybe go and think about it and come back. It was a long journey.

He asked me one day if I would adopt him. I didn't know how to answer that, because I didn't know how to adopt anybody legally, I'd never done it before. I asked him why he would want somebody to adopt him, and he gave me as a reason that one day when he gets married he would like to have a dad to be his best man, and that I was his dad in spirit, and I might as well be his dad legally.

I had some ambivalence, but not much. I wondered what the process involved. I wondered what it takes in law to be a father, what kind of scrutiny I would be under, and I wondered if I would be seen as qualified at the end of the process. I found that it was much more simple than I thought. Reading what the adoption papers say, that's something that the father of a natural-born child doesn't go through. It's pretty awesome the way it reads. "Henceforth, now and forever, Sean so and so will be known as the son of Mickey so and so." It's the kind of thing that sticks in your mind forever.

Even psychologically, the person adopting and the one being adopted go through many challenges. In the first euphoria of it, it's almost like a love affair, nothing can go wrong; you're only for that person. But as time goes on, things get back to normal. For instance, Sean didn't call me "Dad" for a very long time, and I'm a traditional person.

One of the turning points in our relationship was when his "former dad" gave him $100 for Christmas. I kind of felt diminished when I got a call from Sean saying, "Well, Mickey, my dad gave me a hundred dollars for Christmas." I paused when I heard it, and I came across to him. "I'm not the dad of your dreams, am I?" He said, "What do you mean?" I said, "You know, the way I understand it, young men have a certain image of their dads." I said to him, "I'm not flamboyant enough for you, am I? You'd like to have maybe a Beverly Hills banker, maybe somebody in their fifties that still drives a Porsche, maybe wears lots of gold, and be something like you see on TV?"

I said to him, "How many young men in your life do you

know where a man my age stepped in and they had another chance to have another dad?" I said, "God may not have given you a movie star, and He may not have given you somebody from a famous, rich family, but He gave you a city man, rough around the edges, like me. But I do love you, and you do make a difference to me. I didn't really know my parents until they were gone. Will you have the same experience, will your life be better when I'm no longer here? Why don't you really see me for who I am, as I see you for who you are? I'm not looking for a summa cum laude, and I'm not looking for somebody to make me proud. You be the best 'yourself' you can be, you acknowledge me as your dad—I could have no higher ambition in my lifetime."

He stopped, and it was perhaps sinking in. Then I said to him, very bluntly, "My friends call me Mickey. Seeing that you're not my friend, but my son, if you can't call me Dad, please hang up, and don't call me at all." The following day the phone rang, he said, "Hi, Dad, it's Sean, how are you today? I hope you're feeling better than you were yesterday." For several years I've been called Dad and that's the way I want it, that's the way I like it.

I think of myself as a catalyst. If you could take somebody like Sean and turn him into an honest citizen . . . and I'm not saying I turned him into one, but I helped him to understand himself so he could be turned on to himself. I gave him a little something more, a little something to think about. His girlfriend tells me I saved his life. I wasn't trying to save his life, but I saved both of our lives, and enriched our lives. I see some great changes. I tried to encourage him for a couple years to go back to school, and he would have none of it. And now he's gone back to school, and he's got the equivalent of an associate of arts degree.

Several years went by and I never thought it would happen again, but I adopted two more. I began to work with a young man named Jesse. He and his wife Mary invited me for dinner. At that time she was thirty years old, and he was twenty-eight. They had children; some were older that they had from individual relationships, and they had two that were theirs. Mary mentioned to me, "My children don't have a creditable grandfather. You seem like you would be the kind of grandfather they would need."

Was I flattered? Of course I was. Was it an ego thing? Sure, it was that too. Did we immediately make plans to adopt them then? No. They invited me for Christmas and the holidays. The kids started to refer to me as Grandpa. But as I got to know them, with all their positives and negatives, it seemed to me that perhaps they needed me, and I needed them. They had been rejected many times in their lives, and so have I.

Jesse had a father who unfortunately was an alcoholic. He didn't pass much on to him in integrity and wisdom. And Jesse needed that, and God knows he still does. Mary's dad passed away in his fifties. He was her biological dad, but I don't think he was much to look up to. He indulged himself in many affairs. He was, from what I understand, perhaps a drug abuser, and also perhaps a drinker. He lived fast, and he died young. I don't think he appreciated what he had, and I don't think she felt appreciated by him. So, as an adoptive father I don't try to take the image away of their original fathers, but I give them a chance, and they give me a chance, to have a second time around.

Jesse's mother is still alive. She asked Jesse, "Why would you want another father in your life? You already had one." I think maybe she was a little hostile to me to start out with, and so was Mary's mother. But I have infinite patience. I let them get to know me better, and made it very clear to them I'm not going to obliterate the memory or the fondness they might have for their biological parents. This is not who I am.

I saw in Mary somebody fine in their generation: a good cook, a loyal wife, a great mother, somebody who ran a business, somebody who lived a clean life. I respect her a lot. She's a wonderful daughter; she's one of the jewels in my crown. For instance, Mary is somewhat overweight, and she thinks she's not beautiful, and yet in my opinion she is. I try to transfer my values to an overweight woman who is really beautiful inside and out, and tell her, "That doesn't amount to a hill of beans. But the fact that you are a loyal wife, the fact that you are a wonderful mother—now, why didn't someone like you exist for me in my generation? But maybe that's where the Lord might come in—I wasn't forgotten. I couldn't have you when I was young, so I have you as my daughter." And that really makes a wonderful thing.

Mary seemed really enthusiastic; Jesse I wasn't sure of. I didn't want to give him a dad he didn't hold in high esteem. Because Jesse is an impressionable young man, I didn't want to saddle him with somebody that he couldn't feel comfortable with. The reason he's adopted is he asked me. A long period of time went by and he said, "By the way, I think it's time we need to go to court, isn't it?" And that's how it went. So I figured that I would let him ask me, and he did, and here we are. But it's nice to have him call me on the phone in the morning and say, "Hey, Dad, this is your son, and I just want to leave you this message." He'll call at home and say, "Hi, Dad, I just called to say I love you." And I have to play it back once in a while to see if what I heard is really right. It's nice, it's an extraordinary feeling.

And I found that when you give children a grandfather they didn't have, you get rewards. It's wonderful to have them call on the phone and ask me something in history, like how did Abraham Lincoln come to create the Emancipation Proclamation. I can answer their questions. Do we need to vote? Yes. Do we need to pay our bills? Yes. Do we need to be wise in what we buy? Yes. I try to give advice where it's welcome. And I try to be smart enough to hold my peace where I know it wouldn't be welcome.

After I adopted Mary and Jesse Father's Day came, and as a rule nothing much happens to me on Father's Day. And that morning nothing happened, and I thought nothing would. So, the phone rang, and it was Jesse and Mary and they wanted to see me. They took me out to dinner, and bought me a brand-new suit. It was a beautiful suit, and I'm sure it cost them good money. But it was the thought that really counted, that's what really made the difference. And I thought to myself, What an extraordinary experience.

So, what better way to establish a relationship than to have a legal adoption? Nobody could shake it. It's like a marriage, it's like a commitment. You can be good friends, you can call yourself Dad, and "This is my daughter" and so forth, but I have a piece of paper to prove it, and they do also. I know that they're my kids, and nothing can take that away from us; beyond a shadow of a doubt, that's written in stone.

As a middle-aged man I find that the adoptions made me better adjusted as a human being, and I think it did the same for them. Because I'm fifty-seven years old, and I don't want to be alone all my life, and yet I can't live their lives. I don't want to shrivel up to be a bitter old man. I still have a need to love, and to be loved in return.

I think it contributes a stronger family unit to society. It reduces the chance of having too many dysfunctional people out there. But in any adoption, it can go south also, because like a marriage there has to be a give-and-take. I knew them well enough to know that they probably had certain diminished parts of their character. I can't say that they never told me a lie, because that's not true. I can't say that they didn't do things that I didn't hold in high esteem, all of those things. But I didn't want the perfect people, because I'm not perfect either. We make many mistakes; I've made many mistakes. Did I ever lie in my life? Sure I have, because I was too young to understand. Did I ever swipe a candy bar out of the store when I was a kid? Yes, I did. I did all of those things. You accept each other for what you are—your positives, but you know there's going to be negatives. I mean, we're only human.

So, am I a good father to these kids? It depends on how you look at it. I don't have a ton of money to give them. But I care about them. I love them. I stand by them. I try to nourish their intellect, and I'm there when they need me. I'm not a fly-by-night. And I'm willing to tell them when I don't like something, and I'm willing to accept their rejection when they feel they don't like something. I don't think there's ever a time that I say to myself that they're secondary children because they're adopted. They are my children; there's no question.

I hate to see a human being wasted, and it's easy to do. When we're born they ship us off to school, and maybe a teacher is overwhelmed by too many students, and both parents need to work. Who are we by the time we reach twenty-five? Most of us don't know. TV tells us what we should have, and what we should eat. But do we ever take five minutes of the day and ask ourselves what we really think, who we really are, what our essence will be when we're no longer here? Will any of this make a difference? That's what I've tried to do—I've tried to make a difference.

I'm not trying to go back to "Ozzie and Harriet"—those days are gone. But values are not there, and that's why I admonish my children, I say to them, "Maybe getting things the hard way is the right way, maybe standing up to authority and saying, 'No, I will not, because this is not right' is the right thing to do." I showed them a little independence, that I'm willing to stand up for what I believe in. My question to them is, "Have you done all you can do today for the family unit?"

I've had people come to me and say, "You know, Mickey, you have a knack with kids." And I say, "No I don't. I'm blunt, I'm belligerent at times, I tell them just what they don't want to hear. I have values that maybe they don't have." Like a boss once said, who I cussed out many times, "You know, Mick reminds me of a prophet of the days of old. He's grim, he's hard-hitting, but he's fair and he'll look after you." So, there are three souls in the world that perhaps I touched in a certain way, and maybe my grandchildren also. And maybe when I'm no longer here I will have given them something in their minds to be there for them.

I feel like a pioneer in a sense, because I don't know anybody that's done the same thing that I've done in adopting adult children. It makes me feel good; that's my garden. Maybe I didn't flourish in other people's gardens, but I say to them, "You know, I've been rejected many times; you have too. Welcome to my garden. Where you can be the best you can be, or you don't have to, it's up to you, but maybe something I may impart to you may be of some value."

And how do you convince a kid who's been kicked around of any of those things? The best thing you can offer is that you want to be their real father, and you can be that by legally adopting them. That's why I reached out to some of these kids, and I really love them as my own. If I had to give you a day-to-day synopsis, there were great failures among some of these relationships. But overall, so far it's been quite a success. It's something that I wouldn't change. If I had it to do over again, I would.

People know my story, but they don't know quite how to take it. Here we are defending the family unit, and here we're blazing a new trail that yes, you can adopt an adult, you can create another family and it could be something special. Does it contribute to society? How can it not? It's a noble thing, and it's a thing that you don't have to be touched by Divine Providence to do. You're fighting, you're fighting for some-body's soul. That's what it's all about.

I think the process is a good one. Even though they're adults, they're still young and I see the need for it. I think in the future we'll see a lot more of this kind of thing. Maybe by people reading about these experiences, it'll work for them also, or at least they'll be willing to try. These relationships mean something, and they can be sanctified by making them legal. The paper adorns what your relationship already is, be-cause we live in a society, and society likes commitments.

We don't know where we came from and we don't know where we're going on this very short visit here. The power of doing good makes such a difference, doesn't it? It's like the old Diana Ross song, "Reach out and touch somebody's hand. Make this world a better place if you can." And we must, we must.

Update

MICKEY'S FAMILY CONTINUES to grow; he would like to adopt again, and is also now the great-grandfather of a new baby girl.

Comments

MICKEY'S ADOPTIONS ILLUSTRATE just how flexible the definition of "family" has become. With the high divorce rate and the increasing number of blended families, single-parent house-holds, gay unions, and couples who remain childless by choice, the American family has undergone a revolution in the last fifty years. Nontraditional families are now closer to being the rule than the exception.

The beginning of that change came with the invention of a cheap and readily available birth control pill in 1960, and continued with the legalization of abortion in 1973. Perhaps not coincidentally, the divorce rate tripled between 1960 and 1982, and by the 1970s single motherhood was neither shock-ing nor rare. New family frontiers opened as assisted repro-ductive technology became almost commonplace, with sperm donation, egg donation, in vitro fertilization, and surrogacy becoming a billion-dollar industry by the 1990s. During this period adoption, too, began its evolution, from the secret, shame-ridden agency adoptions of the past to the open, choice-driven independent adoptions of today.

Mickey had suffered before his new concept of family emerged—first, a failed marriage, and later a thirty-three-year-old son who stopped speaking to him for reasons that are unclear. Then Mickey found something that struck him dif-ferently than anything ever had before: a fourteen-year-old runaway named Sean. Mickey's life began its transformation with their first meeting. Their relationship evolved from the need of both to have a deep, familial bond with another per-son. It was not preconceived on either of their parts, but grew naturally, and only because each of them was able to under-stand that families could be made, could be re-formed, despite the painful failures of one's first or even second family.

It was Sean's remark, "Tell them I'm your son," that planted the seed for pursuing adoption in Mickey's mind. It identified a need and desire on both their parts, and set the wheels in motion for the eventual adoption.

Because Sean was over eighteen years of age when Mickey adopted him, the correct procedure to build this new and legal family was adult adoption, a little-known and underutilized way of adopting. In fact, there are no national estimates or statistics kept on the number of adult adoptions that take place each year. Adult adoptions are easier, cheaper, and faster than infant adoptions, requiring no home study or state investigation. They rest solidly on a foundation of the mutual wishes of the parties. There are certain limitations; for example, the adoptive parent cannot adopt more than one unrelated adult each calendar year. Another requirement is the approval of the spouses, if either the adoptive parent or the adult adoptee is married. The court also wants information describing the length and nature of the relationship. More interestingly, the law demands something in adult adoptions that it requires in no others—a statement detailing the reasons why an adoption would be in the best interest of the prospective adoptive parent, the proposed adoptee, *and the public*.

The state assumes all children are better off in a loving, stable home environment, but adult adoptions must be explained and justified to the court before they will be approved. In my petition to the court for this adoption, I explained that Sean had been adopted as an infant and returned to the state when he was fourteen by his adoptive parents, and told of his inability to live in group homes and of his life as a homeless runaway. I described the ways in which Mickey had been a stabilizing influence in Sean's life—helping him find a low-rent apartment and a job, encouraging his education—and argued that society is benefited whenever familial bonds are created and strengthened through the law. An adult adoption is not approved without the judge being convinced that the parties are sincere, their goals legitimate, and the adoption's benefits to the public concrete.

Mickey didn't stop his family-building efforts with Sean. He met Jesse and Mary, a couple who each had fathers who because of alcoholism and other personal problems never finished the task of raising their children to maturity. Mickey felt that these "children" of twenty-eight and thirty were still in need of a father, of security, and of guidance. He soon brought them into his family in just the manner an adoptive parent would in adopting a much younger child: with plans and dreams to help them, and treating them in all ways as his natural-born children. He says, "As an adoptive father I don't try to take away the image of their original fathers, but I give them a chance, and they give me a chance, to have a second time around."

In Mary's petition to the court I said, "Mary states that she needs a dad, one that she can look up to and depend upon, one who can be a good role model for her and her children." In Jesse's petition I said that he and Mickey ". . . wished to make a formal acknowledgment of the depth of their relationship and of Mick's relationship to the entire family. The public benefits from such adoptions because of the greater family stability given from the legal status conferred. They also act as an inspiration to others who find themselves lacking a strong family structure, letting them know that affirmative action can be taken to change and enrich one's life."

Mary and Jesse understood that not only did they need a father, but their children needed a grandfather. As a grandparent Mickey serves many functions, not the least of which is sharing the knowledge of a lifetime with his grandkids. "I found that when you give children a grandfather they didn't have, you get rewards." His role is twofold: He's a parent to parents who still need advice, solace, and stability, and he's a grandfather to children who need the loving hands and wise words of a grandparent. Mickey has simply and poignantly expressed these mutual bonds by saying, "I still have a need to love, and to be loved in return." On the practical level, he adds, "It reduces the chance of having too many dysfunctional people out there."

It takes an open mind and heart to make the leap from adopting an infant or child to adopting an adult, and Mickey's example leads the way with a family-building technique that most don't know exists. Mick's children ranged in age from twenty-four to thirty-three when they were adopted. There are millions of young adults in this country like them who haven't finished growing up, or who grew up without the benefit of a father, a mother, or siblings and still yearn to be part of a family. Mickey's experiences not only serve as a model of what can be done at any age, but also help to shatter and rearrange the normal view of adoption and awaken people to the possibility of helping themselves and society through adult adoption.

Consider the problem of the older children in foster care who graduate at the age of eighteen to nothing—no waiting family, no home, no job: and a frightening future. These children can find those things with people like Mickey, who will take them into their lives and finish the task of parenting them. In the last two decades the child welfare system has intensified its efforts to protect children, making it easier to take them from their parents and place them in foster care, while making it harder to actually terminate the rights of the parents of those children. This has created a huge population of "social orphans." Large counties like Los Angeles with foster care populations of as high as fifteen to twenty thousand are experimenting with independent living homes for foster kids who were never adopted and are now eighteen years old and have no place to go. With the creation of these homes the state is acknowledging its failure, admitting that these young people have not been prepared and are in no way capable of being self-sustaining adults.

Assumptions were made years before that these kids were unadoptable. If viewed from the vantage point of those wanting to adopt infants and toddlers, that was certainly true. But there are those people who would welcome the opportunity and the challenge of adopting an adult. The mentoring programs that are so encouraged now, like Big Brother and Big Sister, are versions of family relations, and are extremely valuable, but lack the commitment and legality of adoptive relationships. A more important, lifelong solution could be found by developing programs to introduce these young people who are still in need of parents to people like Mickey who want to adopt them.

Independent adoptions serve the needs of pregnant women and those wishing to adopt infants; public agency adoptions are most successful serving the needs of children from the time they are toddlers to the age of eight. Those older than that are usually resigned to the fact that they will never be adopted, and never be part of a family. But they do not have to be denied this most essential part of life; they can help themselves as adults to live out their dreams of family. Adult adoption will always represent a small portion of adoptions, but its numbers can be increased through the mere knowledge of its existence and an understanding of the benefits it provides. It serves people as diverse as Sean, Jesse, and Mary—everyone from teenage runaways to stable married couples. The flexibility of it adds to its effectiveness and attraction. Adoptees don't have to live with their new adoptive parents if it is impractical or if they don't want to—Mickey has never lived with his adopted children, but they function as all families with grown kids and grandkids do, coming together for the pleasure of each other's company and for special occasions.

Social systems and laws tend to lag behind the needs of the civilizations they serve. This book is about that very subject—how the needs of children, birthparents, and adoptive parents are poorly served by our adoption laws and attitudes. Mickey's experiences made me realize that if little-used and underappreciated laws such as adult adoption could be dusted off and seen in a fresh and imaginative way, we wouldn't have to always wait for legislative changes for help to arrive. Whether through chance meetings like those of Mickey and his adopted children, or through state programs that introduce graduating foster children to parents, these groups of people can avoid going through life without a family, or with one that is fragmented or dysfunctional. They must simply be open to the fact that adoption is not just about babies, toddlers, and young parents—it is about families. And with examples like Mickey's, stereotypes can be eliminated and doors opened that will help many, many people to find a place where they can be a loved and valued member of a family.

11

Three's a Charm

SUSAN

An adoptive mother

"Those memories will always be sad and painful; I
don't think they will ever go away. But the more I do
remember them, the more I learn from them and the
prouder I become of myself and how strong I was
through it. I did survive, where I didn't think I would."

I had my tubes tied when I was about twenty-two,
twenty-three years old. My mother had my sister when I was
seventeen, and she didn't really want another child. I ended
up being the surrogate mother because I was at the age of
having all the motherly instincts, and thinking it was so neat
and wonderful. There were a lot of things I couldn't do because I had to take care of my sister. So on one hand I developed an understanding of how difficult it is to be a
mother—it's not like playing dolls, it's a lot of work. But I
was really kind of resentful and turned it internally. I built up

this wall saying, Well, if this is what it's like to be a mother, I don't ever want to be one.

When I married my first husband, he had an eight-year-old son by a previous marriage. His first wife didn't want him anymore, because she was going off to join a commune somewhere. So he got custody of this little boy that he'd had very little contact with. We had just gotten married and now we had a ready-made family. My husband didn't really want to play daddy, he wanted to be the buddy, he wanted to be the good guy. The child was in tremendous turmoil—he really needed some guidance and some controls. I'd end up having to be the bad guy.

The combination of the two things caused me to decide never to have kids. I didn't have that drive to be a mom yet. I didn't do well on birth control, and my husband wouldn't get a vasectomy. At the time you think, Oh, this marriage is forever. I have a son and it's all I want, I don't want any more.

A lot of people tried to talk me out of getting my tubes tied. When you're that age you think you know everything and what's right for yourself, and the more people tried to talk me out of it the more determined I got, that this is the right thing for me, leave me alone. Come to find out later, I probably wouldn't have gotten pregnant anyway because I had an emergency appendectomy when I was about eight years old and the doctors who did that surgery did not do a very good job. There was a lot of scar tissue and my ovaries were pulled up behind my uterus, so there was no way they were even working or in contact with the tubes.

It wasn't too much longer after that that I got a divorce. The freedom that having my tubes tied provided me was really kind of a bad thing as well as a good thing, in that I was able to go out and become very promiscuous and not really have to worry about it. I really didn't give it a second thought as far as having a family until I was getting close to thirty.

Gordon and I—my husband now—had become really good friends. The more we dated and fell in love the more we started talking about a future together; and one of the things that we both said was that we wanted children. He was willing to adopt. I had already dealt with the fact that I could probably never have children, so my only choice would be adoption and I was OK with that. I didn't want Gordon to be falsely convincing himself that he was OK with it when maybe deep down he would always wish that he had his own child.

It was difficult because he was saying, "I don't care, it doesn't matter to me." But I felt that possibly he was only saying that because he really loved me and didn't want to lose me. I said, "Well, I want to have surgery to un-tie my tubes before we get married and see if it's going to work, before I can make a decision of, Yes, I'll marry you." It was a success and then we got married and that's when the next phase started.

I got pregnant right away; I miscarried. The first miscarriage was so traumatic because I had already been through the surgeries and everything and I was really thinking positively, that this is going to work, we're going to be a family. We were on cloud nine and really let ourselves get carried away. We had a big family announcement with champagne and the whole thing. A week later we had the miscarriage.

I got pregnant again right away and miscarried, and we had four pregnancies and miscarriages fairly quickly. As soon as we had the second miscarriage, we decided to go into an infertility program. We had to argue to get into one. They said, "Well, we really don't take women until they've had at least three miscarriages; we don't consider you being infertile until then." I was telling them, "Look, I'm thirty-three years old, I don't care if I've had only two miscarriages, I want to get into this program now, because obviously there's something wrong."

They found out that I have this antibody problem. I get pregnant, I conceive, the egg attaches itself, but then my body evidently kills it off. The therapy, at the time, was not approved by the FDA or whoever has to approve it. For you to get into the therapy program, you pretty much have to sign yourself off, saying, "Yes, I understand that I'm a guinea pig and it's OK if they do this to my body." I felt that even if I didn't get pregnant that I was providing the world with another statistic that could benefit future women.

This is the interesting thing about infertility; probably all the women who've been through infertility go through this. You want to be pregnant so bad that you're willing to overlook what instinctually, inwardly, you know is wrong because you have to believe in somebody, you have to believe in something. These are the experts, these are the people who are supposed to know. So you tend to say, "I'm not going to listen to myself, I'm going to listen to these people because they know what they're talking about." And you continue on and on and on until finally you've banged your head against the wall enough to say, "OK, this isn't working. Something's got to give here."

I was so exhausted, I said, "I just can't do this anymore. I can't look at another surgery, I can't look at another test; I'm just tired of this." Gordon agreed. This had gone on for about six years. We said, "Forget it—this isn't worth it."

It put a big strain on our marriage, as any fertility program will—more so at the beginning than in the latter part, because you have to do the ovulation thing and know exactly when you're ovulating. You call your husband up at work and say, "Please come home, honey, really quick, it's got to be now." It becomes a job. You look at each other like, "Ahhh, do we have to do this like this again?" There's no spontaneity, it takes all the passion away.

It was a relief to finally have just come to a point of decision and no longer be in a position of hope. Although at the time I didn't realize what we would be getting into as far as the emotional end of adoption, it was such a relief to be done with all the needles and poking and prodding and start doing something that we knew would eventually bring us a baby.

I was really excited about finally taking a step. The first thing that we did is we got our adoption resume going and we advertised in some minor newspapers; we got no response. I was nervous about doing that because I'm real easy when it comes to first impressions, I'm a very gullible person. I was afraid of being taken in by someone that was unscrupulous and was going to try to take us for whatever we were worth.

We found our birthmother, Marilou, through another ad. I went to Montana and picked her up and drove her out here, Marilou and her dog. I thought she was nice; I enjoyed her company. She was a lot of fun to be with, other than she had a fairly foul mouth and she was also very prejudiced, very racist. I was uncomfortable with that because I'm not that kind of person, but I wasn't judgmental of her, given where she grew up and where she was raised.

At that time, Gordon had just taken a job and relocated, and I stayed behind trying to sell our house. It was fine to have her living in our house, because I was by myself. But it was really not a good idea to have her come out, because once she got here, she did not like it here. She didn't like the people, she didn't like the area, she didn't like people with money or people that had things that she didn't have. She couldn't understand why people would live like that when there's people that don't have anything, and exploit themselves and their money by having such huge, disgusting houses. She would just go on and on about it, she was so angry at anybody who had money. I remember taking her to the beach, and she hated the beach, she hated the smell of the water, she hated the fact that black people were allowed to be out there on the beach. She hated where we had to take her for her prenatal care. She felt dirty going there, she said.

In getting to know her I found that her way of operating was that when things started not going the way she wanted them to go she would just pick up and disappear. She had creditors from all over looking for her. And she had a lot of really interesting scars on her body that, to me, looked a lot like burns or how a child sometimes'll pick at themselves until they bleed.

She would not express things that were personal to her at all. She would rarely share the pregnancy with me. I think a couple of times she told me when the baby was kicking, but other than that she didn't want me to talk about it. I remember we were in a place where there were some books and there was a picture book on the development of the fetus. She just thought that was totally disgusting. She wanted to be put out during the birth because she didn't even want to look at it, she didn't want to see anything about it, she didn't want to see the baby after birth. Not because she didn't want to become attached to the baby, but because it was a gross thought to her.

I really wanted this baby so bad I was kind of overlooking things. She continued to smoke, she continued to drink; these two things bothered me, but I thought, "That's OK, we'll get through it." It kind of balanced itself out enough so that I could tuck the negative things aside and try not to pay too much attention to them.

I don't know if she developed to a point where she got to know Gordon and me enough that she didn't like us. I wonder often if the reason why she didn't want to give her baby up to us is because she didn't want her baby to be raised in California. But we had this big fight that kind of ended the whole ordeal, and that's when she said she was going to go home, and her old boyfriend came and got her.

When she left she gave me a hug and said, "Everything

will be all right, don't worry about it." When she got back home she called and said she had got there safely and everything was fine, and that she'd talk to me soon. A week or so later Gordon and I called and talked to her to find out how things were going, and you could just kind of hear it in her voice that she was just being businesslike with us. Gordon asked her, "Have you changed your mind?" And we explained to her that if she had, that was fine, to please tell us because, you know, we wanted to be able to get started looking for another baby. She insisted no, she hadn't changed her mind. But I think both of us knew by the tone in her voice that she had.

I sent her a package with some clothes and some candy and a bone for her dog, and just some fun stuff. The package was returned, not to me, but to our lawyer, with a note saying she had changed her mind and decided not to place the baby with us. I called after that because I wanted to confront her; I wanted to have closure. She answered and I started talking to her and she said, "This isn't Marilou, Marilou's not home." I said, "Marilou, I know it's you, I can tell by your voice it's you." She denied it, and denied it, and I said, "Well, whether it's you or not, I have something to say," and I pretty much said my piece as far as how I felt about the way she handled the whole situation.

Because in the meantime, we had lost out on another opportunity for another baby because of her game-playing. The biological clock was really starting to tick and I was just angry at the lost time, the lost money; I felt used. It brought back all that stuff from the infertility treatments, of just going through all the stuff and not having anything at the end. I had gone into the adoption process knowing full well that these things happened, but truly believing that, OK, we're going to find a birthmom and we're going to find a baby and it's all gonna be happily ever after. And that's not the way it happened.

In not having any way to deal with this and trying to figure out a way to get my frustrations out, I just calmly took a photograph of her and put it in the blender. It does sort of help you to regain your sense of humor, which is really, really necessary when you're going through all this, the ups and downs of this roller coaster ride.

It wasn't very long after that that we found Carla, our second birthmother. But there was the possibility of her baby having Tourette's syndrome [since Carla suffered from it]. How it affected Carla is when she was a child, she would do the dog barking, she was very hyperactive, she would say things, blurt things out, naughty words. They got her onto drug therapy which got it under control. The Tourette's also caused her to be slightly slow as far as her ability to learn.

We decided to go ahead and go through with the adoption. We felt that even if the child had Tourette's we would deal with it. We really liked Carla, although she was kind of a closed person; it was real difficult to get anything out of her. The birthfather was in jail for assault. She had befriended someone else who was in jail who, if I remember right, was convicted of murder, and had become very good friends with him. She didn't see that as a problem, having friends that were in jail. I think that the crowd of people she was hanging around with was a pretty rough crowd, including the birth-father. I think she was going through a real rebellious phase and that she just really had a total disregard and disrespect for people she considered adults.

We brought Carla out here, but she didn't want to come out alone, so her mother came with her. We liked her mother a lot. Her mother seemed to be very open and what we felt was very honest about Carla and Carla's personality and talked a lot to us about Tourette's syndrome and how it affected Carla. The whole time Carla was telling us how she was so positive that this was the right decision, and her mother seemed to reinforce that, saying that she was a little party girl and wasn't ready to be a mom. We were thoroughly convinced that she fully intended to go through with the adoption.

After the baby was born they were both insisting they were happy. In fact, Carla's mom was so excited about the whole procedure and how warm and fuzzy it made her feel, that they were really doing this wonderful thing for a couple who was not able to have a baby, that she decided that she wanted to become a surrogate mother! We walked away from that whole situation feeling positive and thankful.

We took the baby home, and they flew back to Santa Fe. From all indications, everything was fine. She was getting on with her life, she was going to go back to school, she was going to get her body back in shape. I sent her a picture of Joshua when he was three days old that was a gorgeous picture of him. I've often wondered if in getting that picture and having a lot of family and friends tell her he's such an adorable baby, how could you give that baby up, that something clicked, something happened. I don't know if it happened at the hospital when she held him and if she lied to us at that point about wanting to go through with the adoption, I don't know if it happened when she got home and the hormones kicked in—I really don't know. But at some point she decided she had made a mistake and wanted the baby back.

He was probably about a month and a half old, something like that, and just out of the blue I got a phone call from her girlfriend, who said to me, "This is Carla's friend. She's decided she wants the baby back. We'll be down on Monday to pick him up." I said, "No way. I don't know who you are; I don't know if this is true. If Carla wants this baby back, then she can damn well call me because I'm not taking your word for this."

When Carla called, I talked to her and I tried to talk her out of it. I told her that if she was going to be a parent then she better start being an adult and acting like one, and part of being an adult and being a parent is dealing with your problems head-on and taking responsibility for what's happening and not sloughing them off on girlfriends. I told her I absolutely would not deal with anybody else but her.

We wanted to buy some time by forcing her to take us to court to get the baby back. We felt that by buying time she would change her mind, but she didn't. She was a determined young lady and wanted the baby back and took it to the end. Once we finally got the court date, and she had gotten a lawyer, we realized that she was serious. She had done all the paperwork necessary, she had figured out a way to get to

California, and we realized that it was really going to go through. We decided to forgo the court hearing and meet with her at a social worker's office and just hand the baby over that way, which was absolutely the worst day of my life.

That morning Gordon and I were choking back tears the whole time and I had to get the baby dressed and get him ready to go and drive down there. When we got there the social worker took us into a separate office. She really didn't want us to meet with Carla. Gordon and I were so angry we felt she needed to face the reality of what she was doing, we wanted her to see how torn apart we were. I don't know if it was a revenge thing or what, but we really wanted her to understand the depth of pain that she had put us through.

The social worker was not pleased with that decision, and neither was Carla's lawyer. Carla walked in and brought her father with her. We explained in as much depth, as quickly as we could, what Josh likes and dislikes, how he liked to be held, how he liked to sleep, what his favorite toy was—all those basic necessities that she should know to be able to take over being his mother. Then Gordon handed Josh to her father.

The part that really bothered me about the whole incident is that when she walked in she never touched the baby, she never showed any facial expression like she was so pleased to finally see him. The whole time that we were there she never held him. If I had been away from my baby for three months and I had gone through all this to get him, and really, really wanted him badly, the first thing I would have done when I walked in was gone over to touch him or kiss him or something positive. But there was nothing, absolutely nothing from her.

I pretty much fell apart at that point and the social worker pulled me out of there because she didn't want to put Carla through that, which is probably fair, but I wanted her to see how much I was suffering. Gordon started crying then as he had to give Josh his last hug and hand him over. Then we insisted that they sign a paper stating that he was in good health, because we didn't want any kind of lawsuit coming back at us saying that there was something wrong with him or that we had abused him or anything. Her lawyer didn't want them to sign this, but we were not going to leave there without that piece of paper signed. Finally, thankfully, Carla's father stepped in and said, "Look, we know Susan and Gordon are good people, we know they took good care of Joshua, we know he's healthy and he's fine. We don't have a problem with signing it."

It's good for me to remember, because I can look back and say I went through probably the worst day of my life and I survived. Once I got through that I realized there was absolutely nothing in my life that could happen that could be any worse than that. I feel like I can stand up to people and say, "Look, you cannot hurt me, I have been hurt as bad as I can. What you're trying to do right now is not hurting me so don't waste your time." Maybe before I wouldn't have had that strength. I would have bent over backwards to make things right or to fix it or put myself aside. Those memories will always be sad and painful; I don't think they will ever go away. But the more I do remember them, the more I learn from them and the prouder I become of myself and how strong I was through it. I did survive, where I didn't think I would.

Gordon and I talked about it a little beforehand and, both of us having been through losses in our families before, kind of understood what the process was that's involved in losing someone and going through the grieving process. We came to an agreement that we would help each other to grieve and get through this as quickly and as healthfully as we possibly could. The first thing we did was come home and have a really good cry; we probably cried most of the day. We had a little name for it—we decided to call it a "spell." So whenever I was having a spell I would go and tell him I'm having one, and if he was feeling strong at that point he would hold me and listen and let me say all of the irrational, hateful, angry things that had to come out, rather than holding them in. Later he would come in and say, "I'm having a spell," and I would try to do the same for him. So, we tried really hard not to just toughen up and keep the chin up and sweep everything under the rug and put on a happy face.

We took time off work, and I had my sister call all of my family and let them know what was happening and ask them not to call. So we had a few weeks of no visitors, no phone calls, and spent the time with each other and helping each other grieve. We did get cards, which were really nice, and that was very helpful. I think our families felt helpless, which they would have felt whether they were able to speak to us or not. But they understood that we needed time to be alone and we needed time to just cry it out, and not to have to talk the whole story through with person after person after person.

If I had known from the very beginning that there was absolutely no way she was ever going to let us keep Joshua, I would have preferred to go ahead and give him up and get on with it. Because that last month was probably the most painful month of my whole life, of day in and day out wanting to be with him and hold him and spend as much time as I could with him, but on the other hand afraid to hold him and spend time with him for fear I'd become even more attached.

I have convinced myself that Carla just really wanted to be Josh's mother, that she was sorry she had made the decision to place him for adoption. I think that the lies began in the very, very beginning when she was telling us that she was a hundred percent positive and all that. I think she probably wasn't sure to begin with, or at least at some point before the baby was born she became unsure. Once it got closer to the actual birth I think that something clicked in her. Her mother was the only one who knew she was pregnant; I think she was afraid of people finding out the truth and condemning her.

We made one phone call to Carla's mom after Joshua went back, just to find out if he was OK. We found out that Carla had quit speaking to her mother and moved out and moved in with her father. While she was living with her father she found out that he was into drugs and dealing drugs. To her credit, she didn't want Josh growing up in that kind of atmosphere, even though she had her own room, she had a nursery for him, she had anything and everything she wanted. She didn't need to work to support Josh and yet she didn't want him exposed to the drug world, so she swallowed her pride and called her mother, and talked it out with her and moved back in with her. I think that must have been very difficult for her. So I have to give her credit for trying to do the right thing.

It was probably into the second month that we finally said, "Look, being parents, even for only three months, was the greatest thing that we have ever experienced. We don't want to go through life not being parents; we don't want to spend a lot of time doing what maybe other people would think was an appropriate amount of time to grieve." So, against the wishes of a lot of family and friends, we decided to go ahead and start looking again. I'm so glad we did, because it was probably only a few weeks later that we got the call for Ian.

I was in the process of putting a new resume together when we received a call about another birthcouple. As it turned out, they'd taken our resume home, along with a few others, and looked through them and picked us.

We made a date then to get together, and the meeting was tremendous. We hit it off right off the bat. We had so much in common. They want children in the future, but right now wasn't an appropriate time for them. They didn't feel that they could afford it; they didn't feel that they wanted to take time out from their education and their goals to do that. They'd really thought this through—this wasn't just a whim, it wasn't something that they were just looking into. It was a decision that they made, and they were going to stick to it.

From the beginning the birthmother was adamant that she

didn't want to have the baby in a hospital, she wanted to have him at home. When they told us this of course we were terrified, to say the least. Part of my reasoning behind being afraid is that I had been a volunteer for a little girl who was a home birth that had gone bad, who had some just horrendous physical and mental disabilities. My first instinct was, "Oh no," and then my second instinct was, "Well, OK, if this has to be then I want to know everything I can about it."

Once I spoke with the midwife, I felt relieved, although I don't think that I was convinced that this was a hundred percent A-OK—you know, there's always that little percentage of chance that things could go wrong. She seemed really well informed and experienced at what she was doing. She did not accept any clients that were even marginally difficult pregnancies. She wouldn't accept smokers, she wouldn't accept anyone who, once she had accepted them, had to be put on any drugs that could cause difficulties in delivery; she would pass them on to an OB and not accept them as a home birth.

We met the birthparents in December, and Ian was born three months later. We had conversations every once in a while to see how the pregnancy was progressing. Diana, the birthmother, and I would have some wonderful conversations. We would talk about philosophy, about her goals for herself, about our past experiences. She and Scott, the birthfather, were both aware of what we'd been through and were very sympathetic with that. Because of that, I think, they were much more forthcoming with a lot of information. She was nineteen and he was twenty-three. But to speak to them you would think they were in their thirties. They were just so levelheaded and so mature, it was really refreshing.

The birth was the most exciting thing; it was so wonderful to be there. To have it in the home was such a great experience, because it was so relaxed. Diana could get up and walk around if she wanted to. Gordon was what we called "The Iceman"—he was in charge of taking care of the crushed ice for her. Whenever she needed crushed ice, he would feed it to her. I was in charge of helping her hold her head up to push. Her sister and Scott were on either side of her and helping her hold her knees when she was ready to push.

Once Ian was born, the thing that they did, which they don't do in hospitals, they put him on Diana's stomach and didn't cut the cord for fifteen or twenty minutes. They got him cleaned up and wrapped him up in warm blankets and then took care of Diana and made sure everything was going well. Once Diana was taken care of we went back to Ian and got ready to cut the cord and get him bathed and dressed.

You would think that once he was born Gordon and I would want to say, "OK, he's mine, cut the cord, get this separation going." But the whole process of having the home birth and being there was such a bonding experience for all of us. We really wanted Diana and Scott to have as much time as they needed to deal with letting go. Not having Ian ripped away from her right off the bat was really comforting for both of them. It wasn't in the least scary for Gordon and me.

We took Ian out and I breast-fed him right off. [Susan had spent the previous two months pumping her breasts several times each day to prepare for this.] He was less than an hour old. Diana got a little something to eat and got herself cleaned up and comfy in the bed with Scott. Once Ian was fed, we took him back into the room and left him with Diana and Scott and let them have as much time as they wanted with him to hold him and love him and talk to him and say their good-byes. Once that was over, they called us in and said that they were ready.

It still brings tears to my eyes, the good-bye that we had. Ian was only about four hours old and we all had a really good, long talk. We told them how much we loved them and what a tremendous gift they were giving us and that we would never forget that. They said they viewed us as giving them the gift, because we were giving their child a wonderful home and a wonderful life and things that they just didn't feel that they could provide for him. They felt that the giving of the gift was mutual.

We left it that they would take the time they needed, and when and if they were ready they would call us and let us know to what extent they wanted to be involved in Ian's life. It was maybe a month or so after he was born that we got our first phone call. They wanted to know how he was doing, they wanted pictures, and it's gone really well.

You would think that, given what we've been through, once this baby's born I would want the consent to the adoption signed and I don't ever want to have anything to do with that woman again. But I really don't feel that way, and never have. I want Ian to grow up knowing that he is adopted. I want him to grow up knowing that he was given up out of love and not abandoned. I think that the best way for him to know that is to know who his birthparents are. They're such sweet kids that I would love for him to know them, and for him to know that they love him and they care about what he's doing and how happy he is and how healthy he is and how he's doing in school and how he's doing with his friends. And the best way to do that is to keep them in his life.

They are due to come up in the next month, and we're looking forward to it; I think it's going to be wonderful. I didn't want to impose this as a demand on them because I know how difficult the decision is to put a child up for adoption. So, out of respect for their feelings we left the decision up to them. We told them that we were more than happy for them to be a part of Ian's life, as little or as much as they want, that their family is also welcome to be a part of his life as little or as much as they feel they can handle.

Although her parents weren't real positive about her choice—they would prefer that she had the child and kept it— they were supportive of her decision. We never spoke to them, although we've left that option available to them—that if they ever want to speak to us or if they ever want to come by and see Ian, that's something that we would welcome with open arms. One of the things that Diana promised me was if she were having any second thoughts after the birth, that she would seek counseling before anything else. The fact that she had already had some counseling prior to her decision to put the baby up for adoption was an indication to me of how mature her thinking process was and how thoroughly she had really thought things through.

They were really so special. One of the things that they said they would do, which they didn't have to do, was to get the consent to the adoption signed as soon as it was legally possible, and they did. They just bent over backwards to do whatever they could to make us feel comfortable and know that they were sure that they were making the right decision for themselves.

I'm constantly amazed at these two people; they're just so incredibly mature and caring and loving that I just really feel that they're angels, that they are angels sent from God to give us our dream, that they really aren't normal human beings. I've asked myself time and time again, Why did I have to go through all the others to get to this point? Why roadblock after roadblock, delay after delay? I really think, metaphysically speaking, that was God's plan.

What Gordon and I gained from our experience with Joshua helped us so much in becoming parents. We needed that experience to be the best parents that we could be. I can't say that we had a bad marriage—we didn't have a bad marriage—but there wasn't that closeness that we have today, having gone through what we went through with Josh. We became such good friends; there is such a deep level of trust. The commitment was always there, but the commitment that we have now is so much stronger. Josh was the catalyst, because without what we went through with him, I don't think we would have leaned on each other, we wouldn't have shown such deep emotions, such giving and nurturing of each other that we gave each other through that experience. As painful as it was, I'm really glad we went through it. I came out of it a better person, with a better relationship with my husband. Life doesn't scare me anymore; people don't scare me anymore.

I'm having a more difficult time dealing with the anger I have over Marilou than I do toward Carla. Having the experience of being a mother makes me able to forgive Carla's need to be a mother, and that's why she wanted Josh back. Taking him back because she really wanted to be his mother is, to me, forgivable. Marilou, on the other hand . . . I never really knew why Marilou changed her mind. Did she change her mind because she didn't like me or she didn't like Gordon? Is it something that's more personal? Putting her picture in the blender was a quick fix—it's like pounding your fist into a pillow or something that helps you release the tension you're feeling right at the moment—but the long-term feelings have never really gone away. And not knowing what happened with the baby—if she ended up aborting it, if she ended up keeping it, if she ended up giving it up for adoption . . . not having those answers makes it hard for me to forgive her.

I've always been pro-choice. We're all here to grow and to learn and everybody has a right to go about their own life the way they feel is appropriate for them. Giving birth to a child is a very big deal, and giving that child up for adoption is an even bigger deal. And to force a woman to go through an experience that she might not be able to emotionally or psychologically handle, I just don't think, from a spiritual standpoint, is fair. I think that every woman has the right to make that decision for herself. From an adoptive couple's point of view I would hope that all women who got pregnant would have the strength to be able to make that choice for adoption. But to be honest with you, I don't think I could make that choice. I can't imagine forcing someone to make that choice if it's not something I feel I could have made for myself. I would have either had to have had an abortion or I would have had to have kept the baby. There's no way that I could have given a baby up for adoption. I could not have done it.

Update

SUSAN AND GORDON have adopted a second child. After a few visits, Diana and Scott decided to keep in touch by phone only, but Diana's parents visit often and welcome Ian as part of their lives. Diana and Scott are now married and planning a family of their own.

Comment

IF SUSAN AND Gordon's story had been only about Marilou's changing her mind, it would have been sad, but not held the poignancy that it did when their second birthmother, Carla, changed her mind as well and the child had to be returned at the age of two and a half months. Susan describes the day their son went back to his birthmother as the "worst day of her life," saying that life doesn't scare her anymore because she has been hurt as badly as she can be. The depth of that type of loss, and the intensity of the pain inflicted, has to be understood by those making the laws, and it is not. There are two things that contribute to experiences like Susan and Gordon's; one is the length of time the birthmother has to change her mind, and the other is the way the law looks at the money given to a birthmother.

First, the issue of time. Until January 1, 2002, a birthmother in California had ninety days to change her mind after the child was born, and she could change it for any reason whatsoever. Including the nine months of pregnancy and the ninety-day postbirth period, a birthmother had an *entire year* to make up her mind. Intentionally or not, that law and those in other states allowing even more time express a common attitude about birthmothers, and that is that they are none too bright or competent. It patronizes them and assumes that they are incapable of making an important decision within a reasonable amount of time. Anyone who has worked with birthmothers knows that not only aren't they stupid, but that they cannot be coerced into consenting to place their children for adoption if they are unwilling to do so.

No birthmother in any state is allowed to sign a binding consent to the adoption of her child until after the child is born. But many states allow a birthmother to give her consent to an adoption after seventy-two hours have passed. My belief is that consent laws should be changed so that a consent *must* be given within a few days after birth. If a birthmother knew, with certainty, that an irrevocable decision had to be made within a short period of time—for example, five days after birth—the decision would be made. With a deadline, a definite cutoff point, the seriousness of the decision would be contemplated more carefully during the pregnancy and immediately after.

In states like Pennsylvania where a birthmother has months before there will be a termination of her rights, the decision can be and is put off for months. In some of the interviews in this book, birthmothers said that after one's child is born, the legalities should be settled more quickly. In fact, I have never heard a birthmother express the need, or desire, for more time. Those women who do need more time always have the choice of parenting their child until they know with certainty what they want to do.

States with months-long waiting periods craft their laws without concern for the effect of that time on the child or on the adoptive parents. There is a consensus among those who have studied infant behavior that a child is traumatized by abrupt and permanent removal from parental care, a fact which does not seem to be considered in our formulation of adoption law. Are we to believe that Susan and Gordon's son, because he was an adopted child and not a birthchild, was not hurt by being taken away from them after two and a half months? Or that because he is an adopted child it is permissible to treat him with less consideration?

Each adoption has the interests of three parties to consider: the birthmother, the child, and the adoptive parents. Neither the child nor the adoptive parents deserve to be treated like second or third-class citizens; they should be treated with the same respect as the birthmother. By shortening the length of time she may change her mind to a few days after birth, we correct an imbalance that has thrown our adoption system way out of kilter with fairness and reality.

The second issue that caused problems for Susan and Gordon is one that comes up in almost every adoption, and that is the question of money. In California, adoptive parents are allowed to assist a birthmother with medical, living, and legal expenses related to the pregnancy. This assistance may start from the time they meet and continue until approximately two months after the birth of the child. The problem for adoptive parents is that the law considers any money given to a birthmother to be an act of charity, and she has no obligation to return that money if she changes her mind about the adoption. It is a system that invites abuse.

The law, in effect, allows any pregnant woman to claim she wishes to place her child for adoption, have all her living and medical expenses paid for several months, and then change her mind with no further responsibility to the adoptive family. In California there is a Penal Code section that makes it a misdemeanor to take an adoptive family's money without the *intention* to place the child for adoption. But intention is almost impossible to prove, and so prosecutions have occurred in only the most egregious cases, like those where a birthmother is found to be taking money from more than one family at the same time, promising them all the same baby.

Susan and Gordon spent a total of $10,000 on expenses for their first two birthmothers, both of whom then changed their minds. They had enough money to try a third time, but many people do not. Those who say adoption is too expensive and available only to the wealthy must examine this condition of adoption. It allows those of modest means to be taken advantage of and left with no money to try and adopt again. Through our current system, we give the birthmother the power to take away the opportunity for certain people to be parents because they have been able to save only enough money to try it once. Our laws treat adoptive parents as though they were rich rather than infertile, and ask them to carry an unfair burden.

A law stating that a birthmother may receive financial assistance during her pregnancy, but only if it is returned if she does not place the child for adoption, is not an effective solution, if for no other reason than the money would be almost impossible to collect. A prohibition on the payment of living expenses is a tempting possibility, but ignores the fact that many birthmothers desperately need financial assistance and would be homeless or without proper nutrition if no help were available. A more plausible suggestion would be to place a limit on the amount of money allowed for birthmother living expenses, perhaps $3,000. To be effective, the limit would have to be the same in each state, so that adoptive parents in states that do not allow expenses wouldn't be rejected by the birthmother in favor of adoptive parents living in states that allow the payment of all expenses.

Susan and Gordon showed great resilience in trying to adopt a third time. If they hadn't, they would not have found the wonderful child—and the wonderful birthparents—that they did.

12

Rethinking Adoption

WITH EVERY DAY that goes by without a change in the current adoption laws, an injustice occurs. It may be the despair felt by a birthmother who doesn't know how to go about finding a good home for her child, or the frustration felt by an adoptive family who spent all the money they had saved on an adoption that fell through.

I believe there are some changes that could help bring about reformation in adoption law and policy. Let's start at the beginning, with the home study. All adoptive parents are nervous about the home study, because they have only a vague idea of what it entails. The social worker who performs your home study gathers general information about your family history, your job, your relationship with your spouse if you are married, your ideas about child rearing, and your plans for child care. The adoptive parents' fingerprints are taken, medical exams are performed on them and the baby, income and employment are verified, and references written by a few good friends. Usually, this is all done during the first six months of the child's life, and includes two meetings with the social worker. (In agency adoptions it is done before birth.)

Can you fail a home study? Yes, but it's hard. If you lie about something important, like a criminal record, or hide a significant psychological instability you will have problems. You might have trouble anyway, as Patrice did, through no fault of your own. Some agencies and social workers still embody the worst qualities of the bad old days of adoption, judging people harshly and taking an unhealthy pleasure in controlling their futures. On the other hand, I know a convicted rapist who adopted, and know of a convicted murderer who adopted, so there is clearly a lot of "flexibility" in the system.

The home study is a brief look at adoptive parents; the social worker doesn't really get to know them and rarely if ever meets the birthmother or the birthfather. But the problem with this picture is not that it is superficial. Remember, only those wanting to adopt are made to prove their worthiness. Convicted felons and garden-variety bad guys, slobs, and slackers are welcome to reproduce whenever the mood strikes them. And making adoptive parents meet too strict a standard would create rebellion. The problem is that the safeguards and screening the home study does offer are done too late; indeed, in independent adoption the process is only begun once the child is already in the home. If the home study were done prior to birth, all pertinent information and any unpleasant surprises would be revealed before anyone could be too badly hurt or disappointed. It would prepare the adoptive parents for the arrival of a baby into their lives by making them examine their ideas about parenthood, discipline, and how they will discuss this adoption with their other children or families. Through this one important change, adoptive parents would be able to go forward and meet the challenges that await them knowing they have cleared that first big hurdle of "passing" their home study.

Additionally, the process takes too long. What could be accomplished in two or three weeks drags on for months. Swifter evaluation is especially important if the rules of the investigating agency or department won't allow a child in the home until fingerprints have cleared. I have seen several adoptive parents lose out on a chance to adopt a particular child because their fingerprint clearances hadn't arrived or some other part of their home study was incomplete. Eliminating the confusion that surrounds the home study, helping people understand exactly what its components are, and doing it in advance and quickly will eliminate some of the biggest fears and obstacles in adoption.

Once adoptive parents have a completed home study, the focus changes to finding a birthmother. Helping a pregnant woman locate a loving family for her baby should be at the top of our society's priority list, but instead we make it hard for her. Remember the relief Bobbi felt when talking about the facilitator she called to help her find an adoptive family: "She came right to my house." For a girl living in a rural, isolated part of California, this was a huge service. But her city-dwelling counterparts have no easier time of it if deprived of the advertising resources that helped Bobbi.

Between fifteen and twenty states forbid local advertising

by adoptive parents trying to find a birthmother (though some of these states allow adoptive parents to advertise if their attorney or agency places the ad). Advertising is thought to somehow cheapen or denigrate adoption, but it is one of the best, most direct options available. Birthmothers and adoptive parents simply don't know where to find each other. If a birthmother had the opportunity to connect with a family in her state through the local media, she would have the benefit of meeting them, as would her family and the birthfather, all without unnecessary stress and expense. Those states that don't allow advertising simply help the residents of other states and penalize their own.

I emphasize the importance of *local* advertising because of the extra costs and complications endured by adoptive parents and birthmothers who live in different states. Adoptive parents who can only advertise out of state must go to the birthmother's state to meet her, or fly her to their state to meet, and they must do the same thing again at the time of birth. Some birthmothers will agree to come to the adoptive parents' state to give birth, but others have never been in an airplane or out of their state, and the idea of going to an unknown city to meet unknown people, much less give birth there, is not only scary, but may be beyond their capabilities.

The laws of both states must be complied with in every out-of-state adoption, which adds thousands of dollars to the cost of the adoption because adoptive parents must stay in the birthmother's state until they have permission to return home with the child. This may take a week or it may take a month. For adoptive parents who already have a child at home, a choice must be made about which parent will stay home with the first child and miss out on being at the birth of the second child. Sometimes work schedules severely limit the amount of time an adoptive family can be away from their home. They may also have to hire an attorney or an agency in the birthmother's state. Determined adoptive parents get around some of these restrictions by advertising in a national newspaper, hiring a facilitator, or posting an ad on the Internet, although none of these choices eliminate the possibility that an out-of-state adoption may be necessary. The use of facilitators is outlawed in some states, tying the hands of adoptive parents even further.

I am pleading with lawmakers to give adoption the respect it deserves by making it possible for adoptive parents and facilitators to advertise freely in all states. I think adoption should be part of our public discourse, not a dirty little secret legislated out of public view. It is a way of building a family of which we should be proud, and which we should encourage. Women will always have unplanned or unwanted pregnancies, and some of those women will want to place their children for adoption. We should stop making it so difficult for them. There is no sound reasoning behind policies that let abortion clinics and adoption agencies advertise, but forbid adoptive parents to do so. Legalizing adoption advertising simply acknowledges the reality that birthmothers and adoptive parents need to find each other, and helps them to connect.[1]

---

[1] To discover what the laws are in your state, contact the American Academy of Adoption Attorneys at (202) 832-2222.

Once adoptive parents and birthmothers meet and decide to work together, it is almost time to relax and wait for the birth—but not quite. The issue of money must be dealt with up front. It's tempting to ban the exchange of money between adoptive parents and birthmothers with the idea that all difficulties associated with it will then be avoided, including accusations of baby buying, unscrupulous birthmothers who take advantage of adoptive parents, and the exclusion of those with modest incomes. But there are two problems with forbidding payment of living expenses to birthmothers. The first one is that it penalizes adoptive parents from states that forbid it, because birthmothers will simply look for adoptive parents who live in states that will let them help her. The second problem is that it hurts those birthmothers who need food and housing to survive. These women and their families should not be punished by our banning the payment of living expenses based on the abuses perpetrated by a handful of birthmothers or on the fear of some adoptive parents that they are going to be taken advantage of; but significant changes are needed.

The laws regulating the amount of money adoptive parents are allowed to give to a birthmother are different in each state. Assistance with medical expenses and attorney fees is almost always allowed. It is the living expenses—rent, food, utilities, phone—where the differences arise and the potential for exploitation is greatest. Susan and Gordon spent $10,000 in travel and living expenses on their first two birthmothers, money that was lost when both birthmothers changed their minds.

They had the financial resources to try a third time, but for many it would have ended their hopes for a family.

I believe birthmothers should be able to receive help with their living expenses during their pregnancy and for two months afterward in all states, but that there should be a limit of $3,000 on the total amount of money they may receive. This would reduce the adoptive parents' risk and help women in need, but it could only work if *all* states were to have the same cap on expenses. If they didn't, a birthmother would simply search for a couple in a state that allowed them to help her financially in a less limited way.

In California, any money given to a birthmother for pregnancy-related expenses is considered an act of charity and is nonreimbursable. In other words, if a birthmother changes her mind, the adoptive parents' money is gone. I think birthmothers should be held accountable for the money they take. There is no one, cozy answer to the problems inherent in giving a birthmother money to help her during an adoption, so I propose a plan with a choice of three options, to be agreed upon from the beginning: 1) The adoptive parents give the birthmother the money she needs—up to $3,000—in the belief and hope that she will place her child. (Adoptive parents assume the risk.); 2) The birthmother agrees to pay back any money she receives if she changes her mind about the adoption, and a judgment can be automatically entered against her if it is not repaid within three months. (The birthmother is responsible for her choices.); or 3) The adoptive parents have the money the birthmother needs held in a trust account until her consent is final. (There is equal responsibility.)

Being able to pick from among these three choices would make for a more balanced and fair relationship between the parties. Choices 2 and 3 would cut down on the number of fraudulent or insincere birthmothers, and none of the options could be construed to constitute "baby buying," as critics are so quick to call any adoption-related exchange of money.

We have to update our attitudes about the relationship of money and adoption. By giving birthmothers help with living expenses, adoptive parents are only doing what maternity homes have always done. But unlike maternity homes, which demand residence, isolation from normal life, strict adherence to sometimes arbitrary rules, and nonacceptance of women who have other children, financial help from adoptive parents gives birthmothers the freedom to continue with their lives without telling them how to live them.

I made a brief reference earlier to the fact that payment of medical expenses is allowed in almost all states. Because a birthmother may withdraw her consent after a birth that adoptive parents have paid for, they stand to lose a substantial amount of money. One effective way for government to lend adoptive parents a helping hand would be to set up a program that pays a birthmother's medical expenses in all adoptions. These expenses are paid by the government today when a birthmother is covered by state insurance, but many times they don't qualify, or don't or can't supply the needed documents. Paying for the birthmother's medical expenses would be the most direct and helpful way for the government to show its support of adoption.

A plan with three options, supported by a nationwide limit

on living expenses of $3,000, will ease the tensions that build up over money and limit the potential for exploitation. If it is combined with a government-sponsored program that pays for birth-related medical expenses whenever an adoption is planned, the door to adoption could be opened to many more thousands of adoptive parents.

Once the baby is born, adoptive parents and birthmothers are filled with emotions they had only guessed at before birth. Previously calm adoptive parents can become tense and anxious, and confident, determined birthmothers can become ambivalent and even hostile. It's only natural; the possibility of parenthood is so close for the adoptive parents, and the reality of parting so near for the birthmother. Suddenly, no one can think of anything but the consent. All the sincere and friendly feelings that developed during the pregnancy can be shattered in an instant if a birthmother decides to keep her child.

The period of time a birthmother may change her mind about an adoption is different in each state. There is no good reason a birthmother in Nevada should be able to sign a consent after seventy-two hours while adoptive parents in Pennsylvania have to wait months to know if the child they are raising will be theirs or not, but that is the system we live with. Every adoption is infused by fears caused by the waiting period—the longer the waiting period, the greater the fears, and the greater the possibility for disruption of a child's life. Gloria had a real scare during her second adoption when after almost three months the birthmother said she had changed her mind. Luckily, what she really wanted was to be able to see her daughter during the next two or three years, something Gloria was happy to allow her.

Because I believe that the child's welfare should take precedence above all else, and that he or she should be given a stable and permanent home within days of birth, I think three important changes must be made to the consent rules: There should be a short and precise period of time during which the birthmother may change her mind; a simplification of the consent process; and equal consent rules for independent and private agency adoptions should be created.

To avoid accusations that birthmothers are not fully informed about their choice, a system similar to California's is effective. In California a birthmother must meet twice with an adoption social worker. At the first meeting, which usually takes place before birth, she is advised of her rights and the consent is explained to her. The second meeting must always take place after birth, because that is when the birthmother signs her consent.

California law currently says that a birthmother has thirty days to change her mind after she signs. The critically important change that *should* be made if we are to use it as a model is that the birthmother's rights should be automatically terminated after five days. If, on the other hand, the birthmother changes her mind within that time, her child must be returned to her within a twenty-four hour period, with the social worker present as a witness.

This procedure would give birthmothers the opportunity they need to talk freely with a neutral adoption professional on two separate occasions, nine months of pregnancy during which to thoughtfully consider adoption, and five days after birth to assure themselves that their decision is the correct one and one they can live with. It would prevent the heartbreaking scenarios in which a child is taken from adoptive parents weeks or months after birth, and would prevent the child from having to suffer the traumatic loss of the only people he or she has ever known as parents. With this limitation, the adoptive parents, the birthmother, and the child are all treated with fairness and respect.

In many states the law pushes adoptive parents toward private agency adoptions by allowing a birthmother a shorter period of time within which to change her mind than it allows her if the family she is working with is adopting independently. Private agency adoptions are thousands of dollars more expensive than independent adoptions, providing this advantage only to those who can afford it. There are no philosophical underpinnings for this discrimination; agencies do not perform better home studies, and they don't provide better counseling for birthmothers than is provided in independent adoption. In fact, they can embody some of the worst abuses in adoption, such as substituting their own judgment for a birthmother's, or deciding themselves when she is ready to consent to an adoption rather than letting her decide for herself. This discrepancy seems to be a historical inequity left over from the time when agencies dominated adoption.

Now, with independent adoptions making up 85 percent of all infant adoptions in California, and with similar percentages in other states, it is even more unfair to expect those adopting independently to wait a longer time for a birthmother's consent than those using private agencies. Giving agencies this favored status is unfair, costly to adoptive parents, and out of touch with current adoption needs. There should be one law, equal in all cases, that governs the amount of time within which a birthmother can change her mind. If I could change only one aspect of adoption, it would be the consent rules. I believe that the child, the birthmother, and the adoptive parents' best interests would all be served by shortening the time within which a birthmother may change her mind to five days after birth, by simplifying the consent procedure to two meetings with a social worker, and by making agency and independent consent rules equal.

This imaginary child and its welfare that I am discussing with such fervor was not created by the birthmother alone. If there is an invisible presence haunting adoption, it is that of the birthfather. He is invisible not because we choose to exclude or ignore him, but because he usually chooses not to participate. Still, his lack of participation does not mean that his rights aren't the subject of many conversations and sleepless nights. This invisible man can dominate and destroy even the most well-planned and executed adoption. When Colleen chose not to tell the truth about her child's birthfather, she unwittingly put the future of that child at risk. In this case, she and the birthfather had agreed to the deception. If she had kept her pregnancy and the adoption secret from him, the groundwork for another Baby Richard case could have been laid.[2]

---

[2]Baby Richard's birthmother was abandoned by the birthfather during her

With the return of *four-year-old* Baby Richard to his birth-parents, based upon a birthmother's lie and a subsequent claim by the birthfather, lawmakers finally began to make some movement toward coupling a birthfather's rights with respon-sibilities. Oregon created a well-thought-out plan governing birthfather rights, and it serves as a great model for other states. That is because the responsibilities and the rewards of potential fatherhood are placed on the shoulders of the birth-father; his rights are protected in accordance with his actions. Oregon demands that he do one of three things to claim his rights as father: file with the birthfather registry, file an ac-knowledgment of paternity with the birthmother, or show that he lived with and supported the birthmother for a sig-nificant length of time during the pregnancy.

Oregon allows time after the birth for one of these three things to be done. Because I believe the stability of the child's parenting and home is of the highest value, I think that it should have to be done *before* the birth. If the birthfather takes no action, then his rights are gone. It is a strict standard, but there must be certainty that when a child goes into a home, he or she is there permanently. If a birthfather does not pro-vide a birthmother with his last name or address, which is not

---

pregnancy; she later lied and told him the baby died at birth. When he learned the truth fifty-seven days later, he filed for custody. The Illinois Supreme Court decided that because the birthfather had been deceived, the adoption was not legal. Richard was returned to his birthparents. In less than two years the birthfather left Richard and his birthmother to pursue a romantic relationship with another woman, and has seen his son only a handful of times since then.

uncommon, then no further effort should have to be made to find him. Rights must equal responsibility in adoption.

Nationwide, only 1 percent of birthfathers challenge adoptions and want to establish their rights. The strictness of the system I propose reflects the lack of interest shown by almost all birthfathers. The serious birthfather will know enough about the woman he is sleeping with to know if she is pregnant or not and will be able to retain his rights through a simple action; the man who has moved or never bothered to give his full name or address or to stay in contact with the birthmother will lose his rights. It is a simple, straightforward approach that puts the responsibility on the birthfather to claim his rights during the pregnancy by taking a simple, straightforward action. It prevents the possibility of another Baby Richard's ever occurring, thus eliminating the needless suffering he and his adoptive parents endured from ever happening to anyone else.

There is one last detail, about women who are married but whose husbands are not the biological father of the child they are planning to place for adoption. Under current law, when a husband is not the biological father and we are certain of that—because he was out of the state at the time of conception, for example—we must still terminate his rights. This is because the law presumes all husbands are the actual fathers of their children. This often causes a lot of pain for both the husband and the wife, and everyone knows it is a legal fiction. Some birthmothers are terrified of their estranged husbands knowing of their pregnancy and adoption plan because they are afraid that it might be used against them regarding the custody of children they created with their husband, or that he will be violent with them. When it's clear that a husband is not the biological father, a declaration by the birthmother to the court, with any necessary proof, should be sufficient to terminate his rights. Avoiding the sometimes prolonged and expensive efforts to terminate a man's rights to a child we know he did not help create eases a burden on both birthmothers and adoptive parents, and brings needed finality to that child's adoption.

The simplest, shortest, and last of the major points I want to make relates to future contact. I said "shortest" because there is really only one change that needs to be made, and that is: All future contact agreements, whether promises of photos or visitation, should be enforceable through the power of the adoption court. Paul and Marc discussed their intention to have the birthmother and her children be an ongoing part of their lives. They are the least likely people I can think of to break a promise, but the law provides little protection for the birthmother if they were to do so.

One of the foundations of a birthmother's decision to place her child is knowing that she will receive photographs of that child each year. Most birthmothers would not choose to work with an adoptive family who would not agree to that. Not a month goes by without a birthmother's calling and asking me, "Where are my pictures? I haven't gotten any in a year!" I always have a hard time coming up with an answer.

Ideally, postadoption contact agreements could be filed with the court that would make all future contact promises legally binding. The jurisdiction and enforcement powers of the adoption court should be able to follow the adoptive parents no matter where they move, something the adoptive parents would agree to at their final hearing in front of the judge. And meaningful sanctions would have to be developed where there is noncompliance. This one, simple change will have a profound effect on the lives and happiness of thousands and thousands of birthmothers and their children.

My belief that the child's rights and welfare take precedence over those of the birthparents and the adoptive parents is reflected in every suggestion I've made. After the child's rights are protected, I think that fairness, responsibility, and generosity should predominate and be reflected as much as possible in the law. The ultimate question is, How can these ideas be transformed into realities? Some of them, like adopting older children or adults, or treating birthmothers with respect and compassion, can be realized through exposing people to different ways of looking at a subject that they thought they knew. This book presents the adoption experiences of its subjects in the first-person voice in order to do just that: to put the reader in the shoes of the speaker and see the world through his or her eyes. Other changes, like shortening the time within which a birthmother may change her mind about an adoption, or birthfathers' rights, must come about through modifications of the laws of each state.

While writing this book and thinking about the traditional ways of reforming law—for instance, through the lobbying of legislators by special-interest groups—I felt a heaviness, a numbness, as though the task were too daunting, the odds too long. Then I began to think about adoption in a new way.

I realized that it is through works of art that awareness is created and passions are aroused, and through which the most effective changes are inspired. It is books, films, music that have the power to make adoption reform a reality.

The furor caused by the publication of *The Jungle*, by Upton Sinclair, led to the passage of the Pure Food and Drug Act. Rachel Carson's *Silent Spring* created the modern environmental movement that gave rise to a wellspring of laws that protect our world. These writers changed things by putting a human face on huge and complex subjects. I have tried to put that same human face on adoption through the stories in this book, in order to provide a perspective that can't be reached by simply reviewing the law.

I am asking every reader to do one thing to increase awareness of the benefits of and problems with adoption. Write or make a film about it, create poetry and plays that examine it, and simply talk about it at every opportunity. It is the groundswell of people charged with fervor and emotion inspired in them by creative works that will finally get the attention of our legislators.

I appeal to every one of you who has been involved in adoption to begin to share your stories, to form groups and take actions that will influence your state laws. To birthfathers who think they were cheated out of raising their child I say, "Form a group, begin a movement to reform the law in a way you think would make it fairer." To adoptive parents who have been lied to and cheated out of their money I say, "Work for changes in adoption law in your state. Demonstrate. Make an abstract legal concept real by sharing your experience." To birthmothers who have been promised visitation with their children only to have it denied them with impunity I say, "Come out of the shadows, declare yourselves, and work for laws that will enforce the promises that were made to you." To all I say, "Contact the media, question the state, the social workers, the agencies on their policies and see if you can enlist them in your efforts to get the laws changed."

I am trying to practice what I preach by writing this book. Thanks to the brave and generous acts of the clients of mine who shared their stories here, I can use their experiences as teaching tools and reach many more people through this book than I could reach in a lifetime as a practicing attorney. That doesn't mean I won't continue to be an activist in my daily life: educating birthmothers, adoptive parents, and hospital staffs; trying to influence the arbitrary policies of adoption agencies; helping birthmothers find safe housing and health care; assisting them to find the words to answer those who would condemn or exploit them. I can also influence adoption by practicing it in a more humane way, by being available to those in need and being personally and deeply involved in each and every adoptive arrangement.

It is a well-worn truism that America is a melting pot. Millions of people of all races, cultures, and beliefs poured into America to give us our celebrated diversity. Adoption has made that melting pot exist within a much smaller structure, the family. People now learn about and accept other races and cultures through the addition of a family member—a child adopted from China or Guatemala, or a transracial adoption. Adoption is the new Ellis Island, the door through which diversity and richness enter our lives, the fire that fuels the new melting pot. This benefit alone should keep us doing all we can to open that door wider and make it a happier and easier one to walk through.

The pregnant women out there who are looking for a loving family to adopt their child, the infertile couples who are allowing themselves to hope once again to be parents, and the gay men and women who have been excluded from having the chance to create a family—all deserve more than we have given them. With imagination, courage, and hard work, the power to change that is in all of our hands.

Randi Barrow received her law degree from Loyola Law School in 1987 and has been practicing as an adoption attorney since 1989. A leading voice in both adoption and fertility issues, she is a frequent speaker at RESOLVE seminars, the national infertility support organization, and has given California State Bar courses on adoption. She has contributed a chapter to the book *Infertility Counseling: A Handbook for Clinicians*. One of her cases was made into a made-for-television movie, *Baby Brokers*. She is a member of the Academy of California Adoption League and the American Academy of Adoption Attorneys.